PERSPECTIVES

A Multicultural Portrait of
The Railroads

By Liza Tuttle

Marshall Cavendish
New York • London • Toronto

Cover: An American Indian watches the celebration as the last spike of the transcontinental railroad is driven home in Utah. With the railroad, more and more European-American settlers pushed westward, invading and carving up Native American lands that lay in their path.

Published by
Marshall Cavendish Corporation
2415 Jerusalem Avenue
P.O. Box 587
North Bellmore, New York 11710, USA

© Marshall Cavendish Corporation, 1994

Edited, designed, and produced by Water Buffalo Books, Milwaukee

Project director: Mark Sachner
Art director: Sabine Beaupré
Picture researcher: Diane Laska
Indexer: Eileen Foran and Valerie Weber
Marshall Cavendish development editor: MaryLee Knowlton
Marshall Cavendish editorial director: Evelyn Fazio

The editors would like to thank Petra Press for her help in the preparation of this book.

Picture Credits: © The Bettmann Archive: Cover, 6-7, 8, 9, 10, 11, 12 (both), 13, 17, 18, 19, 20-21, 22 (all), 23, 25, 26, 28, 29, 32-33, 34 (top), 36 (both), 38, 39, 42, 43, 44 (bottom), 46, 48, 49 (both), 50 (both), 52, 55 (all), 56, 57 (both), 58, 59, 60, 63 (both), 65 (both), 67 (top), 68, 69, 71, 72, 73; © A. Blodgett/Camerique/H. Armstrong Roberts: 74 (top); © Camerique/H. Armstrong Roberts: 75 (bottom); © Charles Phelps Cushing/H. Armstrong Roberts: 44 (top); © Kansas State Historical Society: 67 (bottom); © H. Armstrong Roberts: 31, 34 (bottom); Courtesy of Siemens Corporation: 74 (bottom); © L. Smith/H. Armstrong Roberts: 74 (middle), 75 (top)

Library of Congress Cataloging-in-Publication Data

Tuttle, Liza.
    A multicultural portrait of the railroads / Liza Tuttle.
        p.   cm. — (Perspectives)
    Includes bibliographical references and index.
    ISBN 1-85435-662-3 :
    1. Railroads—History—Juvenile literature. [1. Railroads—History.] I. Title.
TF148.T83   1994
385'.0973—dc20

93-48324
CIP
AC

To PS – MS

Printed and bound in the U.S.A.

CONTENTS

About *Perspectives*

Perspectives is a series of multicultural portraits of events and topics in U.S. history. Each volume examines these events and topics not only from the perspective of the white European-Americans who make up the majority of the U.S. population, but also from that of the nation's many people of color and other ethnic minorities, such as African-Americans, Asian-Americans, Hispanic-Americans, and American Indians. These people, along with women, have been given little attention in traditional accounts of U.S. history. And yet their impact on historical events has been great.

The terms *American Indian, Hispanic-American, Latino, Anglo-American, Black, African-American,* and *Asian-American,* like *European-American* and *white,* are used by the authors in this series to identify people of various national origins. Labeling people is a serious business, and what we call a group depends on many things. For example, a few decades ago it was considered acceptable to use the words *colored* or *Negro* to label people of African origin. Today, these words are outdated and often a sign of ignorance or outright prejudice. Some even consider *Black* less acceptable than *African-American* because it focuses on a person's skin color rather than national origins. And yet *Black* has many practical uses, especially to describe people whose origins are not only African but Caribbean or Latin American as well.

If we must label people, it's better to be as specific as possible. That is a goal of *Perspectives* — to be as precise and fair as possible in the labeling of people by race, ethnicity, national origin, or other factors, such as gender, sexual orientation, or disability. When necessary and possible, Americans of Mexican origin will be called *Mexican-Americans.* Americans of Irish origin will be called *Irish-Americans,* and so on. The same goes for American Indians: When possible, specific Indians are identified by their tribal names, such as the *Chippewa* or *Mohawk.* But in a discussion of various Indian groups, tribal origins may not always be entirely clear, and so it may be more practical to use *American Indian,* a term that has widespread use among Indians and non-Indians alike.

Even within a group, individuals may disagree over the labels they prefer for their group: *Black* or *African-American? Hispanic* or *Latino? American Indian* or *Native American? White, Anglo,* or *European-American?* Different situations often call for different labels. The labels used in *Perspectives* represent an attempt to be fair, accurate, and perhaps most importantly, to be mindful of what people choose to call *themselves.*

A Note About *The Railroads*

Standing on a bluff overlooking the plains of Nebraska, an American Indian could only watch with dismay as the white man's "Iron Horse" broke the stillness of the day with its shrill whistle and clouded the air with its plumes of smoke. To whites on the East Coast, the sight of tracks stretching westward to unify the continent as one United States of America may have been thrilling to behold. But to Native Americans who had once traveled freely throughout the land, the coming of the railroad signaled danger and doom.

Wherever the railroad went, white settlement followed. The white man was eager to put his name on everything, divide the land into states, gather riches from the earth, and establish commerce. Indians wanted to prosper as well, but by living simply off the earthly gifts of the Great Father. As the railroad crawled its way west, these civilizations came into great conflict.

The white man, with his guns and trains and determination to populate the whole continent, eventually conquered the land, if not the spirit, of the Indians. After decades of clashing, verbally and bodily, over the violation of treaties intended to strike peace, and ultimately deprived of their ancestral living, hunting, and burial grounds, the Indians' will to fight was finally drained from them. Sadly, many great native cultures were lost forever.

The role the railroads played in diminishing the Indian way of life is significant. Many Indians tried to comply with the terms of agreement forged with the U.S. government. And yet, when the government betrayed the trust behind its treaties, many Indians attacked the Iron Horse as though by sabotaging it they could halt the advance of the white man and protect their way of life. In its determination to span the continent by rail, the government justified brutal actions against the Indians in the name of "progress." For many, the motive may have been a desire to expand the horizons of a young nation and to fulfill settlers' dreams. But for the influential few who ran the railroads and the government, it was often the quest for power and money.

The lives and destinies of other ethnic groups were touched by the railroad. The crews doing the backbreaking labor of actually building the railroads were primarily Chinese and Irish, as well as other recently arrived European immigrants, African-Americans, and Mexicans who were willing to work for dirt-cheap wages. In most cases, they were paid less than their Anglo-American counterparts for the same jobs. Later, in the heyday of luxury rail travel, thousands of African-Americans were hired to become glorified servants on the Pullman palace cars, for low pay and inhuman hours.

Without the significant contributions of these minority groups, would the incredible undertaking of building a railroad system to unite North and South, Atlantic and Pacific — leveling mountains and fording rivers along the way — have been possible? Without the trade and travel between the states that the railroads offered , would this be the prosperous nation it is today? It's hard to imagine just what the United States would be like today without the legacy of its tumultuous and once-great railroad system.

Track building on the Union Pacific Railroad pushed through the camps and ancestral hunting grounds of the Plains Indians. To lay track efficiently, the workers were housed in three-story sleeping cars.

CHAPTER ONE

The Spreading of Railroad Fever

L ong before the arrival of Europeans on the North American continent in the fifteenth century, Native American prophets foresaw the coming of white men. They had visions in which all the animals were returned to the earth and their own way of life would be changed forever. These visions helped them accept the fate that befell them in the nineteenth century — when the white man killed off the Great Plains buffalo and declared war against their nations. It also helped them accept the fact that they were not responsible for that fate. They told themselves that it was all part of a greater plan.

What these visions failed to reveal was something that would become all too clear to Indians throughout the Americas: that the white man had little understanding or concern for the lives and cultures of Indian America. The Indians' relationship to the earth and its creatures was more intimate than that of the white man, who was interested mainly in conquering nature — and anyone who stepped in the way of his dreams.

And conquer the white man did. While it is impossible to identify any one time or episode as standing out among the countless invasions and insults directed against America's native people, one period is deserving of attention. That time began in 1830, a year that saw the Indian Removal Act signed into law by President Andrew Jackson. This law forced tens of thousands of Indians living east of the Mississippi to give up all rights to the land their people had inhabited for centuries, so that European-American settlements could prosper.

The year 1830 also ushered in a decade that saw U.S. Army troops escort huge parties of the great southeastern nations — the Choctaw, Chickasaw, Creek, Seminole, and Cherokee —

on a trek by foot over hundreds of miles to new lands in the West that had been promised to them forever. Thousands of these forced emigrants never saw the new territory; they died en route of disease and exposure. Of the Cherokee nation alone, four thousand of the thirteen thousand forced to walk what became known as the "Trail of Tears" died on that tragic exodus.

But that was only the beginning of an era that would see removal — and deception — of historic proportions inflicted systematically on American Indians by the U.S. government. From the earliest colonial times, Indians had found themselves forced to move out of the way whenever land appealed to Europeans. But now, the white man wanted to inhabit the western land and build a coast-to-coast empire with the help of a transcontinental railroad. This time, the Indians fought back. Among other things, they were angry about the intrusion of the railroad through lands that had been promised to them by formal treaty. While European-American treatment of American Indians had long been marked by acts of aggression and betrayal, in this era the white man would go back on his word — and betray Indian America — like never before.

The Indian Removal Act set the tone for years to come. Dozens of treaties between whites and Indians would be cast aside, increasingly because the Indians stood in the way of the white man's schemes for profit — schemes that would be realized all the more readily by the growth of the railroad. It is therefore ironic, but not surprising, that in 1830, the same year the Indian Removal Act was signed, the "Iron Horse," which would follow the Indians to the West — and torment them for the next six decades — was just being developed in the East.

The Steam Engine Wins Respect

At the word "Go!" Peter Cooper urged his little one-horsepower steam engine, the *Tom Thumb*, into action, while right next to him on a parallel track, a single big gray horse snorted and stomped and leaped ahead of the gasping engine. Both were pulling a small train of cars filled with passengers eager to witness this contest between horse and engine. The air was alive with taunts and jeers from both sides.

Cooper's engine got up its steam and gradually pulled ahead of the horse — that is, until the final stretch of the thirteen-mile track that ran from Baltimore to a small town known as Ellicott's Mills. Sadly for Cooper and advocates of steam power, a blower belt failed, and the *Tom Thumb* lost the race.

In 1830, a race between the *Tom Thumb* and a horse-pulled train helped prove the power of the steam engine.

The year was 1830, and the leaders of the canal boat and stagecoach industries had challenged Cooper's engine to a showdown, hoping to prove that steam locomotion was an unreliable mode of transportation. Although Cooper lost that race, he proved to a skeptical America that steam locomotion was at least possible — with a few improvements.

As a businessman and inventor with his attention on many projects, Cooper went on to new challenges. But others were determined to prove the success of steam-powered railroads, and they were just gathering momentum.

England Forges Ahead

In other parts of the world, specifically England, steam engines had already been put to the test. The first steam locomotive was produced by an Englishman named George Stephenson in 1814. Stephenson's father was a poor mineworker. His particular job was to run the steam-powered engine that pumped water up from the bottom of the coal pits. George, who was illiterate until age eighteen, studied that steam engine in detail and became convinced that he could develop a bigger engine that could transport goods and people over long distances.

When owners of England's Stockton & Darlington Railroad announced plans to open the world's first tramway, to be powered by horse, inventor George Stephenson convinced them to try his new steam engine instead.

His opportunity came when a group of English businessmen announced plans to build a public tramway between Stockton & Darlington, two towns twenty-five miles apart. The men intended to use horses to pull the wagons until Stephenson approached them and persuaded them that his engine would do the work of fifty horses. They responded by appointing him chief engineer of the Stockton & Darlington Railroad. With the help of his son Robert, George personally supervised every detail of what was really the world's first public freight railroad, officially opened on September 17, 1825. On that day, *Locomotion No. 1* chugged out of its station bearing thirty-five cars and moving at twelve miles per hour. A new era had begun.

The Stephensons were also involved when, five years later, the Liverpool & Manchester Railway opened service as the first public passenger railway. By this time, Robert had introduced his improved locomotive, the *Rocket*, which could haul loads at up to twenty-nine miles per hour. In a competition sponsored by the railroad company, he beat out four other engines in weight, safety, and performance. By doing so, he secured his position as the foremost locomotive engineer in England at the time.

Early U.S. Transportation

The United States had its eye on the developments in steam locomotion taking place in England. Up to this point, the U.S. depended entirely on canals and rough overland roads for all transportation of goods and people. Travel by these methods was slow and cumbersome. Those with more

inventive minds were aware that if the steam engine could prove itself, the possibilities for its use in the United States and its territories were limitless. Others with even larger sights saw the railroads as a way to open trade with Asian markets, since crossing the North American continent by rail would shorten the trip between Europe and Asia considerably. No matter how a nineteenth-century businessman looked at it, a train system extending from coast to coast would greatly enhance the potential

Before the railroads, transportation of goods and people was limited to waterways or to primitive wagon roads called turnpikes. A toll was collected at the gate marking the beginning of a turnpike.

for lucrative trade. Yet most Americans only laughed at the idea.

One thing that no one laughed at was the need for improved methods of transportation between the states. Between 1790 and 1815, the nation's population had doubled to more than eight million. In the next twenty-five years, it would double again. By 1850, there were thirty states in the Union. More and more settlers, most of whom were of European descent, were migrating westward to places like Ohio and Kentucky, and there had to be a way to link them commercially to the coastal cities.

Many primitive roads, called turnpikes, were built at this time, but these were expensive to build, and the tolls collected for their use made them too expensive for most business. Plus, they were notoriously dangerous. Packs of bandits made a living by holding up the coaches that used the turnpikes.

Water was the other alternative. The country was still spellbound by the relatively new idea of canals. In 1817, the New York State legislature

The white man's "treaties": Another word for betrayal

Behind the scenes and well before President Lincoln authorized the building of the transcontinental railroad in 1862, the federal government seemed to have decided where the first transcontinental line would go. In 1853, President Franklin Pierce sent Commissioner of Indian Affairs George W. Manypenny to visit various Indian tribes "as a preliminary measure, looking to negotiation with them for the purpose of procuring their assent to a territorial government and the extinguishment of their title, in whole or in part, to the lands owned by them." Manypenny didn't visit Indians living along either route favored by northern or southern politicians; he visited only those along a central route, between the fortieth and forty-fifth parallels.

Most native cultures did not acknowledge ownership of land, only the right to hunting and living territories, so the white man's idea of having "title" to certain

parcels was imposed on them. From 1854 to 1857, Manypenny signed treaties with tribes such as the Omaha, Oto, Missouri, Sauk, Fox, Kickapoo, Delaware, Shawnee, taking from them huge tracts of land that had been promised to them only a few years earlier for "as long as the grass shall grow or the waters run." These treaties took back 18 million of the 19.3 million acres recently given the Indians. For example, on May 6, 1854, Manypenny drew up a treaty with the Delaware that took away all of their land except for eighty acres to be kept by each tribe member. The government assured them their land would be made more valuable once the railroad was built. Eventually, the Delaware were forced to give up all their land and move to Indian Territory (present-day Oklahoma), where they soon vanished as a tribe.

authorized the construction of the Erie Canal, whose 364 miles made it thirteen times bigger than the longest existing canal. It was to be the connection between two port towns — Albany on the Hudson River and Buffalo on Lake Erie. (From Buffalo, the goods could be shipped further west by boat through the Great Lakes.) The four-foot deep, forty-foot wide canal was finished in 1825 at a cost of $7 million. Its impact on commerce was significant. What would have taken twenty days to ship now took five, at one-twentieth of the cost. It was a major engineering accomplishment.

The U.S. Picks Up Steam

Soon after the completion of the Erie Canal, ten thousand more miles of canals were planned, only two thousand of which were ever built. Problems with canal travel became obvious, especially the problem of freezing temperatures and prolonged droughts. At the same time, railroads were proving more and more successful. They were not troubled as much by bad weather. They could haul larger and heavier loads because trains created less friction on the rails than heavy boats on water, and they could thus go faster. In a very bold move, the state of Maryland granted the first U.S. railroad charter to the Baltimore & Ohio Railroad in 1827.

Ironically, the completion of the Erie Canal helped fuel the railroad fever that was starting to take hold in the U.S. The Erie Canal had made New York City the most important city in the Union because all trade to the West now started from New York, where it could be sent by ship up the Hudson River to Albany, then by the Erie Canal to all points westward. Other cities, like Baltimore and Philadelphia, resented that. In fact, the main reason the Baltimore & Ohio Railroad was chartered was to build a track westward from Baltimore so that the city could compete with New York and the Erie Canal.

Merchants and politicians in Philadelphia, then considered the young nation's banking and commercial capital, were also spurred into action by the threat of competition. In the late 1820s, the Pennsylvania state legislature authorized an ambitious project that would construct a canal-rail link between Philadelphia and the Ohio River to compete with the Erie Canal.

Canal boats loaded with cargo in Philadelphia made their way first by river to the foot of the Allegheny Mountains. There, the cargo was transferred to rail cars and pulled by a system of ropes up a series of inclined planes to gain altitude. Once at the top, the cars rolled down the rails in gradual steps until the cargo reached the Conemaugh

When the 364-mile Erie Canal was completed in 1825, it connected the East Coast to the Great Lakes and was hailed as the engineering feat of the century. Soon, railroads would outshine canals with faster, more reliable transportation.

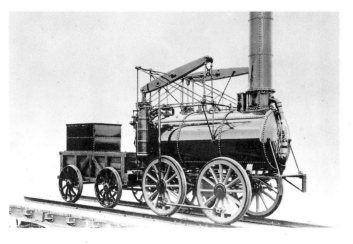

Top: The *Stourbridge Lion* was made in England but imported to the U.S. in 1829. It is now in the Smithsonian Institute in Washington, D.C.

Bottom: The *Best Friend of Charleston* made history when it started the nation's first scheduled steam-powered rail service on December 25, 1830. Six months later, it exploded.

River and continued by water to the Ohio.

City leaders in Charleston, the heart of the cotton-growing South at the time, also realized how they could benefit from a railroad to transport their cotton to northern markets. In 1827, the South Carolina Canal & Railway Company was chartered and in 1830 built a rail link between the cities of Charleston and Hamburg.

At first, the early railways expected that horses would pull wagons over the rails. Some inventive types even experimented with carriages pulled by sails and windpower. Others tried creating energy with horses galloping on a treadmill. None had much success until America's first locomotive, developed by Colonel John Stevens of Hoboken, New Jersey, introduced his sixteen-foot "Steam Waggon" in 1825. It ran at a respectable twelve miles per hour around a circular track he built on his large estate. That was the same year that Stephenson's *Locomotion No. 1* hit the tracks in England.

Importing English Technology

The country's larger canal companies took notice of the advances in steam locomotion. In 1828, the Delaware & Hudson Canal Company sent its resident engineer, Horatio Allen, to England to study the steam engines already pulling large freight loads there. The company instructed him to purchase four engines from Stephenson if he was persuaded of the advantages of such a locomotive. He was duly impressed with the machines, and the four he ordered arrived in the United States in 1829.

The best known of these was the *Stourbridge Lion*. It was tested on track in New York, and problems were quickly discovered. The engine weighed seven tons and was so long and heavy that it jumped the track when it encountered even the mildest curve. Somehow the engine would have to be modified — made lighter and smaller — to be truly efficient. The first man to do that was Peter Cooper, when he came up with his one-ton *Tom Thumb*.

Meanwhile, Allen had left the Delaware & Hudson Company to join the South Carolina Canal and Rail Road Company in Charleston. In 1830, the company built a 137-mile track and presented its first steam engine, the *Best Friend of Charleston*, which could haul six cars with a total of fifty passengers at twenty-one miles per hour. It began service on Christmas Day as the first scheduled rail service powered by steam in the United States. Only six months after its debut, however, an unfortunate accident took place. Troubled by an annoying noise from a safety valve, the fireman attempted to silence the engine by holding down the valve. The engine was silent for a few moments, then exploded into smithereens, fatally injuring the fireman. Many seized upon this tragedy to declare steam locomotion dangerous and unpredictable.

A ride to remember

The third locomotive built in the U.S., the *DeWitt Clinton,* was considered a success when it took passengers on a run between Albany and Schenectady and back on August 9, 1831. One of those along for the ride was a reporter, William H. Brown, who documented the journey:

"It [the locomotive] was a small affair, only ten or twelve feet long, with large wheels, a high smokestack and a central dome. At the rear was an open platform on which the engineer could stand to operate the train. Behind this was a small flat car carrying wood and water for the engine. A leather hose ran from the water barrels to the engine. Three passenger cars, resembling stage coaches, had seats for six people, with room for a few others at the ends. Interest in this test run was so great that the company added five or six flat cars behind the coaches. These had long benches to accommodate the extra people who insisted on taking the ride. This was the first steam train ever assembled in New York state, and a huge crowd gathered to observe its performance.

"When all the cars were filled, the 'Captain' collected the tickets; then he took his place on a little seat on the water and fuel car, blew a blast on his tin horn, and the train started. But not all at once! The cars were joined together by an iron chain some three feet long. As the engine leaped forward, the 'Captain' was jerked nearly out of his seat. A moment later, the first car started with such a jerk that snapped the passengers backward into a heap. A moment later the same thing happened in the second coach, and then, one by one, in each of the following cars. But when all were in motion, the people picked themselves up, resumed their seats and began to enjoy the ride.

"But not for long! The smokestack now began belching forth great clouds of smoke lighted by blazing sparks from the wood-burning engine. The passengers in the three coaches were somewhat protected by the roof of their car, but those on the flat cars behind found themselves in danger of being burned alive. Some had umbrellas with them – for protection against the August sun. They raised these now to protect them from the sparks. But alas! the sparks soon set the umbrellas ablaze, and the flaming objects had to be tossed overboard, where they started fires in the dry grass beside the roadbed.

"Several of the women passengers found their light summer dresses had caught fire, but their neighbors came to their rescue, beating out the small flames with hands and hats and hastily jerked off coats.

"Thus they moved along till they came to the place where the water barrels were to be refilled. The engineer applied his brakes and the locomotive stopped with a jerk. The water-and-wood car banged into its rear end with a crash, and each coach, being attached by the loose chain, smashed into the one ahead. This time the passengers were again piled into heaps, as at starting, only they were all crushed in the front, instead of the rear end.

"When they regained their feet, the passengers went to work to correct the troubles that had beset them. They put out all the little fires that still smouldered on their clothing. Then they took axes, carried on the train to use in replenishing the wood for the engine, and cut down a neighboring fence. They chopped the rails into lengths which they could wedge between the cars to make the train a firm unit, and so prevent the jerks at starting and stopping."

The Beginnings of Railroad Fever

But it was too late to stop the enthusiasm for railroads that was sweeping the country. Between 1820 and 1830, only twenty-three miles of track existed in the U.S., but that number soon grew to one thousand by 1835 and to nine thousand by 1850. By 1860, the U.S. had poured $1 billion into its railroads, one-fifth of which had come from European investors who saw a great chance to make money. U.S. track mileage by that time totaled thirty thousand, more than in all the rest of the world.

Advances in technology helped win over the skeptics of railroading. Soon after the success of Cooper's *Tom Thumb*, engineers everywhere took on the challenge of building a new and improved locomotive. Homemade models of all shapes and sizes were touted as the best yet. One of the most successful was *Old Ironsides*, created by Matthias Baldwin in 1832. Baldwin was a jewelry maker who designed miniature engines to run on a small track in a museum, but he was able to transfer his design to large engines capable of pulling long trains of rail cars. His Philadelphia company, Baldwin Locomotive Works, produced thousands of locomotives over the next several decades and was crucial to the growth of the U.S. railroad industry.

The actual tracks of the railroads were also improved during this time when Robert Stevens designed the T-rail. Instead of a simple strap of iron laid atop a wood rail, with barely any device to keep the train on the track, the T-bar was all iron and actually secured the wheels more soundly to the rail so they were less likely to jump the tracks. By 1840, his design had become the standard in the United States and abroad and is still used today.

During the 1830s and 1840s, hundreds of new lines were built connecting most major New England cities. Critics of railroad travel soon realized that a railroad could make or break the future of their city. Towns everywhere competed for railroad connections, and dozens of companies were chartered to build the short lines between two places with commercial traffic. Unfortunately, these companies often refused to cooperate or use compatible track, so even traveling a short distance could mean changing trains a few times. Before long, the East Coast was a spider web of small, disjointed railroad lines.

The big consolidators

It seemed that as soon as transit by railroad proved itself, new lines were being developed everywhere in the East. Before long, every good-sized city had a railroad connecting it to each of the major cities, such as Boston, New York, Washington, D.C, and Philadelphia. In time, this growing web of railroad track spread into the Midwest as well, with connections to Chicago, St. Louis, Kansas City, and Council Bluffs, Iowa.

Most of the northeast rail lines were eventually controlled by the country's four major railroad companies: the Baltimore & Ohio (the oldest American railroad), the New York Central, the Erie, and the Pennsylvania. The power-hungry leaders of these companies were not above cheating and bullying lesser companies — or each other — for total control. Along with millionaires in the steel and mill industries, they became known as the "Robber Barons" of the Gilded Age. This was a time that saw a tremendous increase in employment, but with much of the wealth increasingly falling into the hands of owners in business and industry.

Rail lines developing throughout the Midwest were initially built by smaller companies, such as the Michigan Central, the Michigan Southern, the Central Ohio, the Ohio & Mississippi, and so on. But by 1895, all these smaller companies were bought out by the same big four eastern companies. This consolidation cut down on competition among the railroads and guaranteed bigger profits for the big four companies, who pretty much ran the show as the nineteenth century came to a close.

But as thousands of settlers moved westward, larger distances needed to be covered, and the idea of "through railroads" developed. A line connecting New York and Chicago was completed in 1853. Philadelphia and Chicago were connected by direct train in 1858. As train service extended into the West, towns sometimes found themselves in a pickle. They had to be able to supply enough business to justify a railroad, and yet it was the railroad itself that attracted more business. By contrast, a city like Chicago, situated on Lake Michigan, was a natural terminus for westward-reaching railroads and was largely created by the commerce it attracted.

Transcontinental Railroad — Visionary Idea or Insanity?

The idea of building a transcontinental railroad that would link the Atlantic and Pacific oceans had been kicked around among America's leaders for decades. But the idea was received with extreme measures of enthusiasm or opposition. Some people became obsessed with the idea but spent their lives trying — and mostly failing — to convince small-minded congressional leaders of the merits of such a project. Until the 1840s, the idea went nowhere.

Several U.S. merchants had made the ambitious trip to the Far East traveling by ship around Cape Horn and were captivated by the exotic goods in the markets of China and Japan. They talked longingly of opening trade routes with Asia, but the time it took to travel there was discouraging. Before long, they began to see that building a transcontinental railroad across North America would shorten the trip dramatically.

Building railroads through the West had its problems. For one, much of the territory was just that — territory — and hadn't been accepted into the Union yet. Also, the Indian Removal Act of 1830 had pushed many American Indians onto reserved lands that were promised to them forever, yet a transcontinental would have to go right through those lands. The U.S. government would have to go back on its promise to them — which it did, all in the name of what the white man called progress. Of course, from the position of the Indians who were dispossessed of what land they had kept from the government, the point of view was certainly different. To Indians, the white man's "progress" just meant more broken promises and more suffering as their lands and cultures were trampled by European-Americans.

Whatever promises had been made to the Indians, the government behaved as though nothing could justify holding up the Union's expansion westward. The nation was growing rapidly, and some means of transportation was necessary to tie the country together. Missouri had become a state in 1820, followed by Arkansas in 1836, and Iowa in 1846. Texas also became a state in 1846 after the Mexican-American War, while Minnesota became a territory in 1849. These new populations all had to be bound together by commerce and passenger transportation.

Still, tallied together, only 1.25 million white settlers were living in the West in 1850 (compared to more than 40 million Americans today). There weren't even enough men in the West to build the railroads, let alone enough people to ride them and keep them financially alive. Still, the government plundered ahead, notwithstanding the Indian "problem."

Geographical problems also hindered railroad development in the West. Much of the western lands were vast prairies without enough trees to provide material for the rail ties. Other areas presented obstacles such as wide rivers, high mountains, or scorching deserts. The railroad companies would have to haul their own materials and their own labor from eastern states, and the cost would be prohibitive. And there were still the loud voices of remaining skeptics who stalled the idea of a transcontinental train system, but mostly for reasons of practical viability, not because they doubted the right of whites to take the land from the Indians. Only a few men in power ever voiced that sort of doubt, but their protests were ignored.

All Those in Favor . . .

Perhaps as early as the 1830s, various citizens were fantasizing about the idea of a railroad to link the two coasts. Many of them published articles in various journals and proposed the idea to Congress, but they were never taken seriously. In 1836, an immigrant Welshman named John Plumbe wrote a well-regarded pamphlet about a "Pacific Railroad." He followed up on his idea by speaking to groups across the country and calling the first Pacific Railroad Convention, held in Dubuque, Iowa, in 1838. As a civil engineer, Plumbe understood how big and difficult a project this would be, and he realistically predicted that it could be done for no less than $100 million (more than three times the federal budget that year). Those who scoffed at the idea to begin with laughed even harder when they heard that estimate.

When Asa Whitney, a wealthy New York merchant, endorsed the idea of the Pacific Railroad, the movement got a big boost forward. For Whitney, the railroad made sense as a way of putting the U.S. in the position of middleman in the trade between Europe and the Far East (a position that could be translated into millions of dollars worth of profit!). In 1844, he had himself just returned from China, where five ports had been opened to trade the year before. He understood well how the trip to Asian markets could be made considerably shorter by going overland by train through the U.S. rather than around Cape Horn or through the Panama Canal by boat.

Whitney's original plan was to use a northern route to connect the Great Lakes port of Milwaukee with Puget Sound. He personally had scouted the route and offered to oversee construction of the railroad if Congress could come up with an initial investment of $50 million.

But his plan met heavy resistance. Pre-Civil War tensions between North and South were getting worse, and southern congressmen were adamantly against a northern route. They argued that more new territory was currently being added in the South, and therefore St. Louis would be the logical starting point of a southern route.

Whitney came back with a revised plan. He offered to raise enough of his own money to begin construction immediately if the federal government would grant him a sixty-mile-wide strip of land along the fifteen-hundred-mile route. He would sell that land to settlers and in doing so, make money for further construction. He would also haul the government's mail, troops, and war supplies free of charge for twenty years, plus regular passengers at half price for the same time period. By 1850, eighteen state legislatures had endorsed Whitney's proposal.

Still, the southern contingent in Congress, and those who felt the federal government itself should build the track, continued to fight against it. As the rivalry between North and South became more and more pronounced, it became increasingly impossible for northern and southern politicians to agree on anything. In 1849, a divided Congress was successful only in setting aside money to finance official government surveys to determine the best transcontinental route. Even that money lay idle for years because of bickering between North and South.

The Great American Desert

European-Americans settling in the East didn't know much about the center of the North American continent — what they called the "Great American Desert" — except that it was wide and vast, with erratic weather and little vegetation. To them it was a barren, insect-infested wasteland where no one in his or her right mind would want to settle. But the western coastal areas were desirable, and to get there one had to go through the desert.

What these settlers and their governments failed to consider was that this "wasteland" was home to hundreds of Native American nations and tribes, each with its own culture, language, and social order. Most European-Americans viewed the native peoples as an uncivilized and dangerous population — an obstacle to the "progress" of western expansion. Yet it was the American Indians who had the most to fear from their encounters with the white people moving through — and sometimes settling in — the land on which they and their ancestors had lived, hunted, and worked for centuries. To the Indians, these vast lands, and all the species upon them, were sacred. They felt their way of life being threatened by the intrusion of these newcomers.

The U.S. government got its information about the central portion of the country from a variety of sources, beginning with the Lewis and Clark expeditions in 1804-1805. In the following decades, the government dispatched several survey crews, including those led by Zebulon Pike and Major Stephen Long, who wrote detailed volumes on what they found. It was not until 1842, when the famed explorer John C. Frémont led a Corps of Topographical Engineers survey, that the federal government began to understand the mysteries of the Platte River Valley in Nebraska and beyond.

A Shoshoni woman named Sacajawea guided explorers Lewis and Clark over the Rocky Mountains on their way to the Pacific Ocean in 1805. Their expedition helped the government learn about a vast continent that was already home to hundreds of Indian tribes and nations.

Kit Carson became famous as a scout for Frémont's explorations into California, but he was also a soldier and Indian agent for the government. Carson was twice married to Indian women and was said to have understood the tragedy of the Indian wars better than most white men.

Frémont's father-in-law, Senator Thomas Hart Benton, had gotten him the assignment; as a politician from the southern state of Missouri, his motive in doing so was undoubtedly to prove that a southern route beginning in St. Louis was the best alternative for the transcontinental railroad. Frémont's famous expeditions caught the nation's attention, partly because he was a vivid writer and detailed the party's experiences for newspaper and magazines upon his return, but also because he hired the famous mountain man Kit Carson as his guide. His descriptions of the wondrous beauty of the West and especially California entranced eastern readers. In one harrowing narrative, Frémont described the 1843-44 expedition he led to find a wagon route to California. When he and his party had tried to cross the Sierra Mountains in midwinter, several of his men froze or starved to death when they got stuck in forty-foot snow drifts. Frémont himself narrowly escaped death to tell about it.

Several events in the 1840s brought the transcontinental railroad closer to reality. The United States became significantly larger with the acquisition of Texas in 1846, and more and more settlers were heading west. Also in 1846, the Mormons made their famous trek to Utah to establish their religious settlement known then as Deseret on the shores of the Great Salt Lake. In 1848, gold was discovered in California, and thousands of Americans rushed to make their fortune digging for gold. Within a year, three hundred thousand people lived on the Pacific Coast. For all these reasons, the transcontinental railway became more urgent and appeared more feasible than ever.

Southern or Northern Route?

Back in Washington, most politicians now acknowledged that a Pacific railroad must be built and soon, but the argument over what route to use dragged on. The Army had sent several surveys out in the late 1840s to explore various parts of the West, but a comprehensive study of all possible routes had not as yet been done. In an attempt to decide the issue fairly, Secretary of War Jefferson Davis finally asked Congress in 1852 for enough funds to send surveying parties on all potential routes. Congress granted $150,000 in 1853 for a ten-month project (the reports were finally filed two years later at three times the cost).

The survey teams explored five possible routes: (1) the northern route, from St. Paul to Seattle (later built by the Northern Pacific Railroad); (2) the Council Bluffs, Iowa, to San Francisco route (a large part of which became the Union Pacific Railroad); (3) the central route, between the thirty-eighth and thirty-ninth parallels, from the Arkansas River to San Francisco; (4) the thirty-fifth parallel route, from Fort Smith on the Arkansas River to Los Angeles via Albuquerque (some of which became the Atchison, Topeka & Santa Fe line); (5) the southern or thirty-second parallel route, from Fulton, Arkansas, to San Diego (parts of which were later used by both the Southern Pacific and Texas Pacific railroads).

These surveys were quite ambitious in scope, but each contained flaws that led to widespread criticism. For one thing, not a single railroad engineer had accompanied the surveys, and important questions of railroad construction were often ignored. Also, the cost estimates based on these surveys ranged widely from $68 million for the southern route to $169 million for the thirty-fifth parallel route, a difference so great that these were also discredited. The reports discussed the advantages and disadvantages of each line, but the overall conclusion was not a very decisive one: All routes were considered possible. While the information gathered was helpful, the debate over where to build the Pacific railroad remained unsolved. This problem, along with economic rivalries and the question of slavery, only helped fuel the flaring tensions between North and South in Congress.

Brigham Young led his Mormons to their new promised land called Deseret, located on the shores of the Great Salt Lake.

Catalyst for Action

When James Buchanan became the fifteenth president of the United States in 1857, he inherited the festering problems of the transcontinental railroad and the disintegrating Union. The two were not unrelated.

Buchanan's first crisis as president proved to him the importance of building the Pacific line — and fast. Brigham Young's Mormons in Utah were becoming quite autonomous and defying the laws of the Union (especially with regard to polygamy, the practice of having more than one husband or wife). Buchanan was forced to send troops to face eighty thousand well-armed Mormons out in the desert, fifteen hundred miles from the nearest railroad terminus. Getting the troops to Utah, with all the weapons and supplies they needed, was a logistical nightmare for the Army, yet they prevailed and preserved the state of Utah. The message to Buchanan and Congress was clear: With a railroad, the effort would have cost a fraction of what it did and would have been resolved much more speedily.

Building the Pacific railroad now had a national defense purpose. With the Union at the brink of collapse, it was critical to make sure that the western states already in existence felt allegiance to the Union. California, for example, had became a state in 1850; it was growing in population — and in wealth! — at a dizzying pace, which made keeping it part of the Union even more important. A railroad could do that, and it could also bring in settlers to help create new states in the country's middle section that more than likely would be antislavery, thus strengthening the North's position. But the ongoing dispute over what route the railroad would take kept Congress at a stalemate for years — until the Civil War broke out in 1861, and southern senators and representatives left Washington to fight with the Confederacy against the Union. Only then — with southern opposition out of the way — could President Abraham Lincoln sign the Pacific Railroad Act. In 1862, Lincoln made it official: The transcontinental would be built along a central route from Omaha, Nebraska, to Sacramento, California.

Building the transcontinental railroad required vast resources, both of men and equipment. At one point during the "Great Race," the Central Pacific had ten thousand men on its payroll.

CHAPTER TWO

The Great Race: The Building of the Transcontinental Railroad

In the middle of the scorching Utah desert, the men building the rails of the Union Pacific and Central Pacific railroads were given barely a moment's rest from the crash-and-scramble pace of their work. Driven hard by the bosses of their respective railroad companies, the mostly Irish and mostly Chinese labor crews were working from opposite directions to meet and complete the first transcontinental railway. For each mile laid, the federal government gave the railroad companies a good sum of cash and land. With only so many miles to go before the rails from east and west would meet, the company that worked faster earned more.

The record for track laying — six miles in twelve hours — was held by the Union Pacific's Irishmen, but only until the president of the UP bet the CP president ten thousand dollars that his Chinese crews couldn't top that. Never mind that the brunt of this sport fell squarely on the shoulders of the common workers while company officers amused themselves. The Chinese were pushed to their limit and succeeded in breaking the record by laying ten miles and fifty-six feet in the same twelve-hour period.

The two tracks were joined with great fanfare on May 10, 1869, at Promontory Summit, Utah, and the country, learning of the accomplishment by telegraph, rejoiced. What had been considered a fool's dream only a few decades before, now became reality. A person could now travel from New York to the Pacific Coast in relative comfort in just ten to twelve days, as compared to an arduous three-month journey by water or stagecoach in the era preceding the railroad.

"Crazy Judah" Makes His Mark

One man whose contribution to the reality of a Pacific Railroad cannot be overstated was a Connecticut-born civil engineer

Collis Huntington (above), Leland Stanford (middle), and Charles Crocker were three of the conniving, money-motivated "Big Four" who built the Central Pacific Railroad.

named Theodore Judah. He was dubbed "Crazy Judah" because of the zealousness with which he promoted the notion of a transcontinental railroad and for his flair as a speaker. He came on the scene when, in 1854, after building several small eastern railroads, he was selected for the job of building a railroad from California's capital, Sacramento, to a bustling gold-mining town called Folsom (also in California) at the foot of the Sierra Nevada Mountains.

Judah built that railroad and then was hired to survey a wagon route across the Sierras to the Nevada silver mines. But by this time, Judah was bitten by the transcontinental bug and was convinced that a rail line could and should be built over the mountains. He was approached by a local pharmacist named Dan Strong who believed he knew the best route. The two men formed the Central Pacific Railroad Company and began looking for investors.

Judah talked up his idea with relentless enthusiasm, in California and in Washington and many points between, but people still weren't ready to believe in it. In 1859 in the halls of Congress, all talk was about the prospect of a civil war, and no one had time for Judah's harebrained railroad schemes. Judah returned to California and tried to interest potential investors in a railroad going only as far as the silver mines in Nevada. Four Sacramento businessmen listened this time and saw in his plan a way for themselves to get rich. These men were later referred to as the Big Four of the CP Railroad. Their names were Leland Stanford, who owned a grocery business and later became governor of California (he also founded the university that bears his name); Collis P. Huntington and Mark Hopkins, partners in a hardware store; and Charles Crocker, a dry goods merchant.

With their financial support, construction began on the railroad. But Judah's sights were still on the transcontinental line. He returned to Washington in 1861 to convince Congress that now more than ever — with the Civil War a reality — a transcontinental railroad line was critical to keep the rich states of California and Nevada in the Union. It took him a year, but he finally persuaded Congress, and in 1862, President Abraham Lincoln signed the Pacific Railroad Act.

The Civil War itself gave the transcontinental railroad a boost. It was the first war fought — and largely won — with the help of the railroad. Moving troops and supplies was much faster and easier with the railroad. The North had quite an advantage over the South in this regard since the North controlled more lines and virtually all the factories making locomotives and rail. Destroying railroad lines played a big part in the South's offensive plans. All the Union leaders began to see how important a railroad could be for national defense and unity.

The Pacific Railroad Act acknowledged the federal government's responsibility to help with such an enormous project. The financial costs would be so staggering that private funding would never be enough. The new law provided generous loans to the two companies it empowered to build the transcontinental — the Central Pacific and the Union Pacific (chartered by the act from an existing line, the Chicago, Rock Island & Pacific, which already had lines into Omaha, Nebraska). For every mile of track built in the lowlands, the companies would receive sixteen thousand dollars; for each mile in the mountains, forty-eight thousand dollars. The act also gave considerable land grants to each company, with the dual purpose of creating income for the railroad companies who sold off the land and of encouraging white settlement of the country's vast midsection. The federal government was happy to find a way to get rid of the land, considered by most white people to be "barren and Indian-infested."

Soon after he saw success in the passing of the Pacific Railroad Act, Judah reached an impasse with the Big Four. While Judah's inspiration was in building the transcontinental railroad, his partners were interested solely in building personal fortunes. In disgust, Judah allowed himself to be bought out for one hundred thousand dollars, and he returned to the East Coast. On the way, however, he contracted the yellow fever crossing by ship through Panama and died within a week — a sad and ironic end for a man fighting to build a railroad that would make traveling through Panama unnecessary.

Theodore Judah threw his heart into his idea of a trans-Sierra railroad, but money for the project came from the "Big Four," who eventually pushed him out of the project.

Moneygrubbers Stall Progress

With the Union Pacific building westward from Omaha and the Central Pacific building eastward from Sacramento, the transcontinental was being accomplished in the fastest manner possible. Or so it was thought. In the first years, the Union Pacific made little progress mainly because of infighting among its appointed directors over who would act as president. Once the moneygrubbing Thomas Durant craftily bought up a majority of the stock and installed himself as president, he wasted additional time figuring out which route was the most profitable for him personally and how to set up a dummy finance company so that most of the government money would end up in his pockets. He did a good job at that. He organized a separate company, the Credit Mobilier, to which he paid large sums, while the railroad company itself went deeper into debt. It was such a successful scam that the Big Four of the CP set up a similar hoax.

A woman's contributions overlooked

One woman whose impact on the transcontinental railroad was never really appreciated was Anna Pierce Judah, wife of Theodore. She faithfully followed her husband on his surveys in the Sierra Mountains for the Central Pacific railroad, sketching and documenting all she saw while living in pretty harsh, wilderness conditions. Of the hundreds of sketches she drew, two were used to decorate the stock certificates of the Central Pacific railroad.

But that was to be her only honor and the only tribute to her husband's significant involvement in the building of the transcontinental railroad. Her husband died before the transcontinental was completed, and no one ever thought to invite her to the ceremony at Promontory Summit. The day the rails were joined was also the anniversary of the Judahs' wedding, and Anna spent it in her home in Massachusetts. She later wrote, "It seemed the spirit of my brave husband descended on me, and together we were there."

The CP men also had other tricks to get more money. They had fake surveys done in the Sierra Mountains showing that the range began much further west than it actually did so they could collect the higher $48,000-per-mile grants. These despicable men were the first "Robber Barons" of the railroads, and they set the example for many to follow in their footsteps in later years.

The Railroad Laborers

Not surprisingly, considering their attitudes toward them, money and labor were two constant problems for the companies building the transcontinental line. Construction was often stalled due to a lack of one or the other. Both companies depended on huge armies of men to build the tracks since all the work was done by hand. At any given time, each company had several thousand men on their payrolls. The work they offered was strenuous, if not downright dangerous, and required living in the "wilderness" for months at a time, often at the mercy of bad weather, marauding buffalo, and angry Indians, who resented the intrusion of trains and traffic on their lands.

Because construction really got under way just as the Civil War was ending, there was a constant stream of war veterans and freed slaves to work on the railroads. The Union Pacific was built by these and by immigrants, especially the Irish, who had come to the U.S. after the Irish potato famine of the 1840s. The Irishmen in particular were known to work hard — and to play even harder. They drank, brawled, and gambled their earnings away in the saloons and brothels that migrated westward along with the railroad crews. These mobile towns were so rough and tumble they earned the nickname "Hell on Wheels." More men were killed by the lawlessness and disease spreading through these ramshackle towns than by the hardships of railroad construction. When the crews moved on, tents and wood-frame buildings were packed up and moved with them. Many cities in the West were started — and finished — this way.

Besides the colorful and flamboyant Irish, the Union Pacific also hired recently freed African-American slaves; some Indians, such as the Shoshoni, Paiute, and Washo; and (when the railroad entered Utah) Mormons. All these workers were part of the well-orchestrated dance the UP construction bosses choreographed for speedy construction.

The Work Method

With so many men and materials required to build railroads and with the distances involved, the Union Pacific bosses devised a "work train" that supplied all the men's needs. A single engine pushed a train of cars, each outfitted for a different purpose. The first car — nearest the point of construction — carried all the necessary tools, followed by a car serving as a blacksmith's forge. The next few cars were much taller and lined on the inside with three tiers of sleeping bunks for the men. Then came the dining car with one table running the length of the car. Eating was a simple affair: at breakfast, for example, the men dipped their coffee cups into a communal urn, ate from tin plates nailed to the table (for the ease of the dish swabbers), then left by simply stepping over the table. The last few cars carried all the rails, ties, spikes, bolts and other supplies. As the cross-country race heated up, the work train was eighty cars long.

Construction on the Plains was much faster and easier than in the mountains. According to one news reporter following the Union Pacific tracks, the crews worked with the discipline of a military operation. On the front line were the surveyors, perhaps a few hundred miles out, who plotted the course of the track. Behind them, the graders' job was to cut through the gorges, build bridges, and level the earth for the track. The main body of the army — the tracklayers — worked as fast as they could. Horse-drawn carts carrying sixteen rails plus all the necessary hardware traveled to the front. Here they were emptied, tipped off the rail, and gotten out of the way for the next load to come forward. Five men grabbed each rail, placed it and measured the width, or gauge, between them, then stepped aside as the spike men began swinging their sledge hammers. The rhythm was fast and unbroken.

During the heat of the "Great Race," Union Pacific "work trains" carried so many men and so much material that they were often eighty cars long.

The Casement brothers, Jack and Dan, led the crews of the Union Pacific. They paced their workers and were constantly enticing them to greater speeds. At first, they set a goal of one mile of track per day and gave each man a pound of tobacco if they met it. Once that became routine, they offered to pay them an extra dollar a day (three instead of two) if they laid a mile and a half. Eventually, they offered four dollars for two miles a day through the scorching Utah flatlands as they raced with the Central Pacific crews for mileage.

The CP Teams

The CP crews were initially made up of frustrated gold-seekers who had emigrated to the West during the Gold Rush in 1848. But the populations in California and neighboring states were limited, so the CP leaders had to find alternative sources. They first tried shipping Irish immigrants from Boston to California, but that became too expensive. During that time, San Francisco had experienced a steady flow of Chinese immigrants (many of whom came to clean up whatever gold was left after the 1849 Gold Rush), and Crocker, one of the Big Four, got it in his head that they might hire the Chinese to work on the railroads, and for much lower wages than their usual laborers. Stanford, the CP president, considered the Chinese frail and strange and scoffed at the idea. Crocker reminded him that, after all, the Chinese had built the Great Wall of China, so maybe they were capable of hard work.

The hiring of Chinese laborers to work on the Central Pacific was not taken well by their white counterparts, who found them "strange" and treated them poorly, sometimes even violently.

After repeated advertisements for labor brought in only dozens of men where hundreds were needed (most preferred trying to strike it rich in silver and gold mines rather than working a tough twelve-hour day), a desperate Stanford agreed in 1865 to hire fifty Chinese as an experiment, and they proved so capable that he launched an effort to import fifteen thousand more from China.

China at that time was in bloody chaos because of rebellions in various parts of the country, and Chinese men were eager to work overseas, at least temporarily. They were mostly young agricultural workers recruited from the Cantonese districts of Sinong and Sinwain and promised big wages — that is, once they managed to repay their passage by ship (about thirty dollars by sailing ship, forty dollars by steam ship) at up to 5 percent interest per month. They were jam-packed aboard ships belonging to the Pacific Mail Steamship Line, often more than legally allowed, and en route, they often became sick from the unfamiliar food and motion. Many also gambled their way across the Pacific and landed in California in far more debt than just for their boat fare.

Once working, their wages were usually about twenty-six to thirty dollars per month, about the same as their American counterparts, but board was not included for them. They also supplied their own food and cooks because they couldn't stomach the meat and potatoes offered by the company kitchen.

Hardly a warm welcome

The trip from China to the United States took thirty-five to forty days by steamer, and many of the Chinese men arrived feeling sick and bewildered by the new culture. Most spoke no English, and there were few interpreters available. Their first challenge was to survive the city's white underclass, who tormented and teased them, following them through the streets, yelling at them, pulling their pigtails, and hurling objects at them.

According to one witness, "They throw brickbats and missiles . . . , and so, often, these poor heathen . . . reach their quarter of this Christian city covered with wounds and bruises and blood, received at the hands of parties whom Chinamen suppose to be fair representatives of this boasted Christian civilization. Sometimes the police have made a show of protecting the Chinamen, but too frequently the effort has been a heartless one, and the hoodlums have well understood their liberties under our sacred guardians of law and order."

As more and more Chinese were imported by the Central Pacific, the situation worsened, and concerned San Francisco citizens formed a Chinese Protective Society that met each ship and provided a special police force to protect the immigrants. Once in Chinatown, they became members of the Chinese Six Companies, an association run by Chinese businessmen that provided legal, medical, and financial services to the new immigrants. From there, they were divided into work groups and sent by riverboat to Sacramento, and then on to the railroad construction sites.

They ordered special shipments of Chinese delicacies, such as seaweed and abalone, from San Francisco, insisted on bathing and changing clothes before their evening meal, and drank huge amounts of boiled tea — all of which the other men found peculiar. Truth is, they suffered far less from stomach and intestinal disorders, probably by virtue of drinking boiled water instead of the dirty ditch water consumed by others.

They were not readily accepted by their fellow workers because they were just plain different. They were shorter and smaller than most European-Americans, usually weighing about one hundred pounds, wore loose blue pajamas and wide-brimmed straw hats, and had a long braid hanging down their back. They never drank alcohol or consorted with prostitutes, and they didn't fight unless provoked. They kept pretty much to themselves. What they did do was gamble, and well. They aroused much suspicion and contempt in others because they usually won.

In most cases, the Chinese spoke almost no English, and they learned their jobs simply by watching and doing. At first they performed the most menial tasks, until, job by job, they were put to the test and succeeded. While they were at first considered incompetent when it came to work, they quickly earned the respect of their counterparts and especially of their bosses. When the crews banded together to demand better wages, the Chinese didn't take part. They were content with their wages and rarely complained.

Each of the men performed different tasks, some more physically demanding than others, some more dangerous. The biggest challenge faced by the Central Pacific crews was the Sierra Mountains. To get a foothold on the sheer granite faces of the mountains, Chinese were lowered in wicker baskets to pick a ledge wide enough for the men with explosives to stand on. Their job then was to blast a path wide enough for the Iron Horse, or locomotive, to chug its way through. Picks and chisels and traditional blasting powder

Playing Russian Roulette with a Swedish explosive

When the Central Pacific crews met with the unyielding granite of the Sierras, no amount of traditional blasting powder could bite into the mountains enough to make the kind of progress CP leaders expected. James Strobridge, chief engineer for the CP, decided to try the relatively untested nitroglycerine, a blasting oil eight times more powerful than powder.

Unfortunately, two shocking accidents told the public all they wanted to know about nitroglycerine. In April 1866, one shipment ordered by the CP bosses exploded in a Wells Fargo office in San Francisco, killing twelve and sending a severed arm through a third-story window. A few days later, a freighter blasted sky high in Panama while en route to California. Fifty people were killed instantly. In both cases, the cause was found to be incorrectly labeled

crates of nitroglycerine, and the federal government ordered an immediate ban against the substance.

The CP bosses craftily devised a way around the ban by shipping its ingredients separately and hiring a Scottish scientist to concoct the explosive in a special mountain lab. Irish laborers were sent to blast rock with the oil until a fatal accident occurred in one of the tunnels. From then on, the Irish refused to use it, but the Chinese, described as more fatalistic, were willing to accept the risk.

No records were kept of how many accidents occurred with nitro or how many Chinese were killed, but it was used until an unexpected explosion resulted in the loss of one of Strobridge's eyes.

weren't strong enough to make more than a dent in the mountains, but an even stronger explosive, nitroglycerine, had just been invented. The nitroglycerine was used to carve tracks and tunnels through the Sierras, sometimes at the less-than-snail-like pace of eight inches in a twenty-four-hour period, but not without killing and wounding many of the Chinese setting the blasts.

The construction boss for the Central Pacific was a man named Strobridge, said to be as ill-tempered as they came. He bellowed and verbally berated his men into submission. The Chinese were afraid of this physically overpowering man, who was often known to settle arguments with his fists. Whatever he asked of them, they did.

The Dangers of Railroading

Railroading was tough work, and besides routine health problems and small injuries, everybody was at even greater risk. The railroad crews often found themselves in crisis due to weather: snow and cold in higher elevations, heat and dehydration in desert areas. The winter of 1866-67 took its toll on both the Union Pacific and Central Pacific crews. Thick, blowing snow stalled progress on the UP lines for weeks, but the CP crews were even worse off. At the highest elevation of the line, Strobridge's men were at work around the clock on the most challenging tunnel through the Sierras, the Summit Tunnel. Forty-four blizzards were counted that winter, one dumping no less than ten feet of snow, and whole work crews were stranded, existing on emergency rations for weeks at a time. With heavy drifting, avalanches posed the worst dangers, and in one incident, twenty Chinese died when their barracks were whisked down the mountainside. No one knows how many others died alone or in pairs after being buried alive.

An additional peril for the Union Pacific crews was the constant threat of Indian attacks, especially by Sioux, Cheyenne, and other Plains Indian nations who were irate over the intrusion of the railroads through their lands. The white man's dirty, snorting "Iron Horse" and the "civilization" that came with it disturbed the peace, spoiled the environment, and drove off the herds of buffalo the Indians depended on for survival. In retaliation, they led raids on the railroad crews that often resulted in heavy casualties on both sides. The heaviest attacks came in 1867 as the Union Pacific made its way across Nebraska and another line, the Kansas Pacific, laid track across Kansas.

To protect themselves, survey parties never went out except accompanied by an escort of U.S. soldiers. Crews began to arm themselves, dropping shov-

The Northern Pacific Railroad was the second transcontinental line; it was completed in 1883 with crews that included some Chinese workers.

The CP Woos the Indians

The Central Pacific line crossed fewer Indian territories than did the Union Pacific. And where it did, the bosses bought their way out of an Indian "problem" by signing a treaty issuing lifetime railroad passes to the Shoshoni and Cheyenne chiefs they encountered and promising that all tribal members could ride the freight cars free for thirty years.

The bosses also offered jobs to Shoshonis and Paiutes, who worked side by side with the Chinese with no interracial problems. Female Indians were also hired, and it is said they routinely showed up the men with their use of the crowbars and sledgehammers. Despite the generally friendly associations between Native American and Chinese laborers, certain cultural contrasts occasionally rose to the surface. Once, while a construction gang of Paiutes and Chinese were working on a grade in Nevada, the Paiutes entertained themselves by telling the Chinese stories about the desert and watching their reactions. According to one tale, the desert was home to snakes large enough to swallow a man whole. During the night, five hundred Chinese fled the camp and headed back to Sacramento. Charlie Crocker of the CP's Big Four had to send men on horseback to chase after the Chinese and convince them that the Indians were just pulling their legs.

els in favor of rifles when Indians appeared. The U.S. government launched several raids in an attempt to drive the Plains Indians north of the Platte River and south of the Arkansas River, leaving a wide strip of land in between for the railroad and white settlements. In the summer of 1867, Army regiments — often led by former Civil War generals — burned villages and killed Indians with abandon. The Indians fought back.

The St. Paul, Minneapolis & Manitoba railroad was built with the protection of U.S. Army escorts, complete with a band. The "skyscraper" cars were bunkrooms for the men.

The federal government later tried to sign treaties with the angry Indians. They succeeded with some leaders, but others were unbudgingly against the railroad. These continued to plan ambushes, destroy rail, and plunder the trains. The U.S. government deployed more infantry to defend the construction sites, and more cavalry to patrol completed tracks, but the war between the two groups continued. General Sherman, believing the railroad more important than any Indian claim to the land, was determined to protect it against such "a worthless set of scamps" as the Plains Indians. Eventually, the white man prevailed, and most Indian tribes were either diminished significantly or forced to move north, where the buffalo herds had already been driven.

The Great Race

In 1867, the Central Pacific had advanced eastward only 40 miles through the Sierras, while the Union Pacific crews had progressed 240 miles across Wyoming. That exasperated the Big Four, who saw government money and valuable land slipping through their fingers. The Great Race, as it has become known, was on. The CP bosses decided to send crews over the Sierras and into

Utah. There, they began laying track on the flatlands during the winter months while the going was so slow in the mountains, so as not to lose time in claiming more mileage for the Central Pacific. The Chinese laid tracks to Reno, Nevada, before they returned in the spring of 1868 to finish the seven-mile gap from Sacramento in order to receive a fortune in government bonds for *consecutive* rail.

The Central Pacific leaders also dispatched surveyors as far east as Wyoming, where the teams bumped into flags and markers already placed there by the Union Pacific advance men. Both companies were after the green and fertile flatlands the Mormons called home, and both signed deals with the Mormons to have them build railroad grades across Utah. The Mormons agreed to both contracts and proceeded to grade two hundred miles of parallel tracks across Utah, one set of which was never used. The CP paid the Mormons twice what they paid their Chinese workers. This money came from U.S. taxpayers, who hailed the transcontinental without realizing how wasteful the Great Race was becoming.

The UP put extreme pressure on its Irish workers to gain mileage through Utah, and instead of making winter camp in 1868-69, they pushed their workers to the limit, paying them double to work in bitter cold, picking at frozen earth and laying track on snow and ice. (The tracks became useless and in need of repair come spring when the ground melted beneath them.) Accidents happened with increasing frequency, but when workers complained, they were goaded on by racial taunts: Would the UP crews be shown up by a bunch of Chinamen? The men continued work at night by moonlight and lantern.

The lure of receiving double pay had little effect, because, in fact, the workmen had not been paid at all for several weeks. The Credit Mobilier had issued Christmas dividends to all its stockholders, leaving the UP itself millions in debt and unable to pay its workers. Brigham Young's Mormon crews hadn't been paid either. Durant couldn't be bothered by this, however, and ordered the crews to continue at breakneck speed. In April, he issued his bet against the CP leaders that their Chinese crews couldn't break the UP record of six miles of track laid in one day.

The Transcontinental Becomes Reality

The U.S. government had never specified where the two railroad lines should meet, and eager to collect all the money and property possible, the companies continued right on past each other, their graded railbeds overlapping for more than two hundred miles. Often the rock debris from one crew's dynamite blasts would rain on the other. Before any rail was actually laid on these portions, the federal government called a halt to the foolishness and set the meeting point at Promontory Summit, Utah.

The day the railroad lines were joined was planned as a grand occasion. The two lines were halted fifty feet from each other so that the final span could be finished with much ceremony. The day was scheduled for May 8 and the CP dignitaries had arrived, but the event had to be postponed two days because Durant's private car had been secretly unhitched in Piedmont, Wyoming. He was being held prisoner by an armed mob of angry railroad workers. Until Durant wired money to cover all back wages due, the workers would not let him continue to Utah. He gave in, and the celebration took place on May 10,1869. With the engines of the two companies nose to nose on the tracks, Stanford and Durant, surrounded by hundreds of onlookers, were to hammer in the final spikes, specially made for the occasion from gold and silver. The holes for the spikes had already been driven, the tools fastened with wire to telegraph the final blow of the hammer. Stanford and Durant had only to tap the spikes into place. They both swung and missed the spikes, but the telegraph operator covered for them and sent the message across the U.S. that at last the transcontinental was reality.

Chinese crews for the Central Pacific spent the winter of 1866-67 nearly buried under forty-foot snowdrifts as they built tunnels through the Sierra Mountains. They were forced by money-anxious bosses to continue work through the winter, digging chimneys and air shafts and living by lantern light. Hundreds died in snowslides.

While the white men shot the buffalo indiscriminately and let the carcasses rot on the plains, Indians killed only the number they needed to survive and made use of the whole animal.

CHAPTER THREE

Prosperity and Trouble

Out on the Kansas plains, buffalo herds like huge dark shadows once roamed untroubled, except for the Native Americans who hunted them and the wolf packs that lived off them. Together, these two predators killed only a tiny percentage of the population each year, and only for purposes of survival. When the Iron Horse entered buffalo country, European-Americans shot the animals left and right, for food and for fun, and their numbers plummeted.

To American Indians, the buffalo was one of the four-legged creatures with which humans shared the earth, a being to whom thanks would be offered whenever it was called upon to give up its life. But to most non-Native Americans, the buffalo had become one of the symbols of the West, a novelty that easterners came to see in its natural environment. Once the western railroads were operating, it became great sport for train passengers to take potshots at the passing animals. They came out by the trainful, with rifles loaded and ready. They shot from moving trains and from stopped trains, dashing about yelling and whooping and leaving the animals dead where they lay. The Kansas Pacific ran special excursion trips during the 1860s especially for the experience of killing a wild buffalo. For ten dollars each, passengers traveled from Lawrence, Kansas, to the end of the line 410 miles west and back, to entertain themselves by shooting as many buffalo as they could.

Upon finding a herd, the engineer would stop the train and let out the would-be hunters. Here is how one passenger, John Putnam of Topeka, wrote about the action in 1868: "Everybody runs out and commences shooting. We failed to bag a buffalo. I did not shoot, having ill defined ideas as to hunting rifles,

which end you put the load in and which end you let it out at. ... But I rushed out with the rest — yelled promiscuously, 'Buffalo! — Stop the train — let me out — there they are! — whoopey — give 'em thunder — no go — come back — drive on.' So you see I helped a great deal."

Professional hide hunters were also at work in the West. They killed the animals and sold the hides to tanneries in the East. The carcasses were dried and the bones were ground to be used for fertilizer. In Europe, the market for buffalo hides — and for buffalo tongue, considered a delicacy — was booming.

On contract with the Kansas Pacific Railroad, William F. Cody, better known as Buffalo Bill, earned his fame by being the best buffalo hunter in the West. In the middle of Kansas, where one herd was so large that a train once had to wait eight hours for it to cross the tracks, the KP railroad bosses, short of meat for their hungry railroad workers, recognized an opportunity. They hired Buffalo Bill to kill a dozen of the huge animals each day to feed the thousands of men at work on the railroad. Cody would ride out on his horse, find a cluster of buffalo, shoot from his galloping horse, and usually in twelve shots fell twelve animals.

Top: The Kansas Pacific encouraged the senseless destruction of the Great Plains buffalo by running trains for thrill seekers. In two decades, the number of animals plummeted from one hundred million to a few hundred. *Bottom:* "Buffalo Bill" Cody was hired by the Kansas Pacific to provide buffalo meat for workers. He could down twelve animals in twelve shots while riding at a gallop.

By contrast, the few thousand animals killed each year by the various nations of Plains Indians were used for food, shelter, and clothing. Not much of a downed animal was wasted by the Indians. They watched in dismay as the white man steamed west in big Iron Horses the Indians called "Bad-Medicine Waggons" and killed the buffalo that the Indians depended on.

Four major herds of buffalo in the Western plains probably contained more than one hundred million animals before 1860. By 1875, all but six or seven hundred remaining buffalo were gone forever. But by that time, so were most of the Indians who depended on them, having been killed, decimated by disease, or chased into northern territory by the white man.

Native Americans vs. the Railroad

The Indians had little trust for the white man by the time the railroads penetrated the plains in the 1860s, and with good reason. Whole nations of eastern Indians had been forced to relocate farther west, leaving behind sacred land and burial grounds. Treaties had been made and broken already. As trains and European-American settlers moved westward, the Plains Indians watched their own ancestral hunting grounds being portioned off and violated.

General Philip Sheridan, a Civil War veteran, was given the task of making peace with the Plains Indians. His approach was this: Any tribes not accepting resettlement on reservations were to be hunted down mercilessly. Building the railroads and cultivating the West for agricultural purposes was considered far more important than the Indians' claim to the land.

The year 1867 was a pivotal one for Indian-Army conflicts. The Plains nations had intimidated the railroad crews enough that they were unwilling to work without a guard from the U.S. Army. Yet a good number of U.S. troops were busy protecting peace in the post-Civil War South. Soldiers stationed to guard railroad crews were often overwhelmed, especially when the railroad workers they were supposedly protecting were spread out over a distance of sometimes hundreds of miles.

Their way of life threatened, the Indians tried desperately to sabotage the Iron Horse. They attacked trains, ripped up rail, and tore down telegraph lines. In one poignant incident, a party of fifty warriors on horseback tried to capture a locomotive with rawhide lariats. They stretched them over the tracks, holding on to each end, and waited for the train. When the train came along at twenty-five miles per hour, several Indians were pulled along and swung into the wheels, where many were dismembered.

That horrifying story may have been a source of entertainment for white listeners, but chances are they weren't nearly as amused when the Indians succeeded in wrecking the trains, which they sometimes did. One particularly well known raid took place at Plum Creek, Nebraska, in August 1867. Responding to a break in the telegraph line, five men were sent out on a handcar to investigate and repair the problem. Unbeknownst to them, a group of Cheyenne had used the wire to fasten a rail tie to the track in an attempt to derail the next train. The men in the handcar hit it first and were quickly ambushed by the Indians. The repairmen tried to get away in the handcar, but the Indians killed four out of the five immediately. The lone survivor, a man named Thompson, was shot in the arm.

Lying quietly on the ground pretending to be unconscious, Thompson was thought to be dead. He heard the Iron Horse coming and might have flagged it off, but the Cheyenne were still around, and he lay still. The train came upon the obstruction and careened into the ditch. The engineer and fireman were killed on impact. Other men ran down the track to warn a freight train that was following close behind. While the Indians were busy looting the wrecked train, Thompson ran fifteen miles to the nearest railroad station to tell his story.

The more the Indians fought against the railroad, the more determined the white man was to impose his will. More and more soldiers were sent to protect the railroad. In 1867, while UP crews were building track one hundred miles out of North Platte, Nebraska, warriors were ambushing groups of railroaders on a regular basis. Grenville Dodge, UP chief engineer, lost his temper after one incident, screaming to his company superiors, "We've got to clean the damn Indians out or give up building the Union Pacific Railroad. The government may take its choice." By 1868, nearly five thousand soldiers

Top: Native Americans, like these Crow Indians, were taken prisoner by Army soldiers for trying to protect their right to live on the lands their ancestors had lived on for centuries.
Bottom: These Apaches, including the famous Geronimo (seated third from right) were captured in Texas in 1886 and sent via the Southern Pacific Railway to a detention camp in southern Florida.

were patrolling the construction sites of the Union Pacific alone. The Kansas Pacific, another transcontinental line being built only two hundred miles to the south, was also heavily patrolled. The U.S. government was determined to take the West.

Yet even as the Indians gave in and were forced northward from Nebraska and Kansas into the Dakotas and Montana, the route of another, northern transcontinental, the Northern Pacific, was displacing them again. The Indians were caught in a no-win situation, despite promises made by the government that each relocation would be permanent. There was nowhere else for them to go. By the 1880s, five transcontinental lines existed: the UP-CP line; the Atchison, Topeka & Santa Fe; the Northern Pacific; the Great Northern; and the Southern Pacific. Each of these lines had tussles with Sioux, Blackfeet, Crow, Arapaho, Cheyenne, and other nations. But the struggles between the Northern Pacific and Sioux Indians in the Dakotas and Montana led to the biggest U.S. defeat during the so-called Indian Wars.

Pawnee scouts

In his campaign against the Plains Indians in 1865, General Grenville Dodge relied heavily on the skills and advice of a group of Pawnees who had chosen to enlist in the Union Army to help fight against their blood enemies — especially the Sioux, Cheyenne, and Arapaho — rather than be sent to prison camps. Known as Pawnee Scouts, they formed a cavalry battalion under the command of Captain Frank North, who had been a trader with the Pawnee and spoke their language. The Indians — about one hundred of them — provided their own horses but wore pieces of U.S. Cavalry uniforms so as not to be mistaken for Indians of other nations and tribes. They were posted along the Union Pacific line in the Platte Valley and were very successful in detecting, thwarting, and defeating Sioux and Cheyenne raids — so much so that they were signed up for a three-year stint.

The Pawnee in general got along well with European-Americans and often lived on the edge of railroad construction sites or other white encampments ready to sell their services, particularly if doing so helped deal a blow to their hated enemies. In addition to their skills as scouts and interpreters, they were willing to entertain parties of white people with mock war dances and buffalo hunts, something visitors from the East or Europe were always eager to see. Eventually, several Pawnees performed with Buffalo Bill's traveling Wild West Show.

Custer's Indian Raids

During the 1870s, Indians continued their attacks on the railroad, and businessmen in the East and Midwest were getting impatient. They wanted to get their hands on the rich natural resources of the West, especially the timber, minerals, and ore necessary to fuel the rapidly industrializing eastern parts of the nation. They lobbied President Ulysses S. Grant to take full and decisive control over all the states and territories in the West. Grant responded by calling in the U.S. Army under General Alfred H. Terry to force the Sioux and Cheyenne onto reservations. Among the troops he sent was the Seventh Cavalry Regiment, under the command of the famous Civil War hero, Lieutenant Colonel George Armstrong Custer.

Custer already had a reputation among Native Americans for his rampage against Sioux, Arapaho, and Cheyenne encampments in western Kansas when the Kansas Pacific line was being built. His orders from General William Tecumseh Sherman on one particular attack were to "destroy their villages and ponies; to kill or hang all warriors and bring back all women and children." Custer and his cavalry disobeyed; they indiscriminately killed all the men, women, and children and burned their villages to the ground.

Even earlier, in 1864, a southern Cheyenne chief named Black Kettle signed a peace treaty with the U.S. government that allowed him and his people to live at Sand Creek, Colorado. To show his loyalty to the treaty, he even flew an American flag over his tent. On November 29, troops surprised the unarmed settlement at dawn and massacred the sleeping Indians. Black Kettle lost his wife and most of his men, but he survived to sign two more treaties with the government.

The second of these was the Treaty of Medicine Lodge. In return for moving to a desolate reservation, Black Kettle and his tribe were to receive supplies and guns to kill buffalo to live on. The government didn't hold up its end of the bargain. Black Kettle appeared at Fort Larned, Kansas, in 1868 to ask for the supplies: "Our white brothers are pulling away from us the hand

The "Buffalo Soldiers"

They were regular Army, they were indispensable in the Union's battles against the Plains Indians, and they were all African-American. They were the Ninth U.S. Cavalry's "Buffalo Soldiers," dubbed that by the Indians who thought the texture of their hair resembled the coat of a buffalo.

Once the Civil War was ended, the Army reduced its peacetime ranks to just ten cavalry and twenty-five infantry regiments. Two of each were made up entirely of African-American privates and noncommissioned officers, but under the command of white commissioned officers. For twenty-five years, these troops fought against Cheyenne, Comanche, Kiowa, Apache, Ute, and Sioux Indians and against Mexican outlaws along the border. More than once, detachments from these Black regiments came to the aid of white troops. As testimony to their talents out on the frontier, between 1870 and 1890 fourteen African-American soldiers were awarded the Medal of Honor.

Also fighting against the Indians, but not as part of the Army, were freed African-Americans who had established themselves as cattlemen of the West. Two in particular, Charley Tyler and Britton Johnson, were apparently known far and wide until they were killed, respectively, by the Paiute in California and the Kiowa and Comanche of Texas.

Indian warriors out-witted cocky U.S. General George Custer at the Battle of Little Big Horn, otherwise known as Custer's Last Stand.

they gave us at Medicine Lodge, but we will try and hold on to it. We hope the Great White Father will take pity on us, and let us have the guns and ammunition he promised us so we can hunt buffalo and keep our families from starving." The government first turned him away, then relented and handed over the promised goods. Black Kettle settled in western Oklahoma and lived off the buffalo there until November 1868, when his encampment was attacked again, this time by Custer and his Seventh Cavalry. Black Kettle and nearly all his men were slain.

Black Kettle and the southern Cheyenne were never a "problem" for European-Americans again, but their allies — the Arapaho, Kiowa, and northern Cheyenne — lost all trust in the white man and waged war more furiously than before against the railroad while they waited eight years to avenge their hatred for Custer.

Their chance came in June 1876, when Custer rode into Montana territory and came upon an Indian encampment at Little Big Horn River. Custer believed himself outnumbered by at most two to one — perhaps 1,000 Indians to his 650 men — and divided his regiment into three flanks to surprise the Indians. What he didn't know was that a war council had been called by Sioux chief Sitting Bull, and 5,000 Indian warriors were present. They rose up and wiped out Custer's entire column in a battle known as both the Battle of Little Big Horn and Custer's Last Stand. According to an Indian veteran of the battle, the fight "did not last long enough to light a pipe."

For the Indians, this was a momentous victory over the white man, but, in fact, it did nothing to stall the intrusion of the Iron Horse, and if anything, it merely made the federal government more determined than ever to extinguish the Plains Indians to the last living soul. Sitting Bull himself fled to Canada after the victory, and he and his people nearly starved during the bitter winter that followed. When asked by a friendly white trader why he didn't agree to live on a reservation, he replied: "Because I am a red man. If the Great Spirit had desired me to be a white man he would have made me so in the first place. He put in your heart certain wishes and plans, in my heart he put other and different desires. Each man is good in his sight. It is not necessary for eagles to be crows. Now we are poor but we are free. No white man controls our footsteps. If we must die we die defending our rights."

Waves of White Settlers Arrive

Much of the impetus behind the relentless siege upon the Indians came from businessmen and land developers anxious to get busy "civilizing" the West —

in other words, making themselves rich by trading goods and property. But they recognized that settlers would be reluctant to come until the threat of Indian retaliation was eliminated.

By the 1880s, the Plains Indians were limited to reservations and were no longer considered "dangerous" by the white settlers. At that point, the railroad could embark on its mission of colonizing the West. And the railroad had a unique role to play as colonizer and land developer in this part of the country. In the West, where the railroad went, settlement followed.

The immediate goal behind the railroads' great push to find settlers was to raise money by selling the plots of land along their right of way. The railroad companies often needed that money in order to continue building westward. The more long-term goal was to help establish the communities that would provide steady business for the railroads into the future. Naturally, the settlers were interested mostly in land near where the railroad stopped, since the railroad was the crucial transportation link between the urban centers of the East and the agricultural and mining regions of the West. Without it, the settlers who established farms and cattle ranches in the West would have a hard time making a living.

As early as the 1850s, the Illinois Central Railroad was involved in a zestful appeal to easterners, recently arrived immigrants, and potential immigrants still living abroad to come to Illinois, where the land was fertile and inexpensive. Advertisements were placed in English- and foreign-language newspapers throughout the East and in newspapers abroad. An agent was sent to Germany to recruit settlers. Posters adorned trains and horsecars in New York and other major cities, and leaflets were printed by the thousands and handed out at Ellis Island, where most immigrants first set foot in their new country. These enticements beckoned settlers with words that often exaggerated the beauty and fertility of land in Illinois, giving them the false impressions that the state was already settled more than it was. Competition was fierce among various states for these settlers, so all manner of salesmanship was employed. It worked: during the decade of the 1850s, 1.5 million acres were sold, and the state's population doubled to a total of 860,481.

The same aggressive advertising techniques were used by the Burlington and Missouri River Railroad to settle Nebraska and Iowa in the early 1870s, to similar success. Land in these states was advertised at eight dollars and twelve dollars per acre, respectively, with interest rates at 6 percent. While these advertising campaigns often claimed — falsely — that a person could earn more money in the West and pay less for necessities, they were also often truthful about the type of person likely to succeed in

Advertisements beckoning immigrants and others to buy "cheap" land in the plains often left out details such as bad weather, angry Indians, and utter desolation, all of which made many settlers long for home.

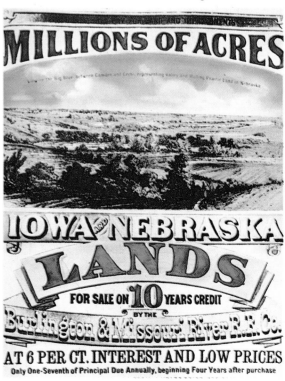

Propaganda wars

"Every foreign labourer landing on our shores is economically valued at 1,500 dollars," said an 1870s U.S. report. Arriving with an average of one hundred dollars for every man, woman, and child, immigrants also contributed to the gross national product once they began farming. One government official calculated that in ten years, the railroads could attract enough immigrants to add $4.8 billion to national coffers.

The various transcontinental railroad lines fought each other for as much of that wealth as they could get. They wooed potential land buyers with exaggerated prose. One ad spoke of "flowery meadows of great fertility clothed in nutritious grasses and watered by numerous streams." Some companies promised ready-built homes (but settlers soon found themselves owing more than they could afford in high interest rates), or free seed for the first year (many complained that the seed was primarily quack grass and weeds).

Some companies actually tried to hijack groups of immigrants who were already headed to another state. One of their tricks was to have their luggage purposely mislaid, so that while they were delayed, company agents could convince them the land they were headed to was far inferior to the land they had to offer. As one of the main transfer stations to the West, Omaha was crowded with land agents for various railroads, making enough promises to make an immigrant's head spin.

Bribery was also widespread. Steamship agents in Europe were sometimes paid for each immigrant they transported, and agents at Castle Garden, where the immigrants first landed in the U.S., would send newcomers to the office of whichever company had paid them the most. It was a dirty business that treated newly arrived foreigners like freight, not human beings.

the new territory. Only those willing to work at hard physical labor — either in the mechanical trades or in agriculture — were encouraged to come, not "persons accustomed to living by their wits alone," as one flier read. Apparently, "men of liberal education" — doctors, lawyers, teachers and other professionals — were in oversupply.

To find these hardy farmers, the railroads looked primarily to northern Europe: Germany, Scandinavia, Britain, and Russia. These settlers were willing to overlook the ruggedness of the weather and territory for the opportunity to own their own land. A particular target, recommended by the U.S. ambassador in St. Petersburg, Russia, were the Mennonites, members of a pacifist religious group, whom he described as "intelligent, industrious, persevering, clean, orderly, moral, temperate and economical." The Mennonites were happy to come, on certain conditions that they successfully negotiated with the governments of Kansas and Nebraska: freedom from military service for at least fifty years and freedom from any taxes to support any military operation. To this day, Kansas has a particularly large population of Mennonites.

Germans and Scandinavians also responded by the tens of thousands to the advertising done by railroad agents, largely because of the desperate shortage of land in these countries. One Santa Fe railroad agent boasted of singlehandedly getting sixty thousand new settlers for Kansas. Eventually, the immigrants began to be treated like merchandise, rather than humans. One agent spoke of being able to "supply several thousand Swedes to be furnished, if ordered now." In the early 1880s, the Northern Pacific had 831 agents in Britain and 124 in northern Europe, aggressively pursuing recruits to emigrate to America. Britain saw an opportunity to send over its poor and wayward souls, and government and charity groups often financed the voyage

The great American sell job

In the race among railroads to attract as many buyers and settlers for their land as possible, all manner of promises were made and broken. Agents described the western lands as though they were already half settled and producing crops as soon as seeds landed in the ground. In reality, many settlers found themselves a day's journey from their nearest neighbor and with land that had little chance of becoming the garden of Eden it was described as, at least not without a lot of blood, sweat, and tears.

To get new settlers on their railroad line, railroad agents promised to help build irrigation ditches, windmills, or barns, but their promises were never in writing and rarely fulfilled. In truth, most immigrant families ended up in sod houses or dugouts and worked the land without producing much in the first year, only to learn that they owed more than their life savings to the railroad. With different languages, cultures, and expectations, many ethnic groups felt very much alone and helpless in America. They had no one to help keep them from being taken advantage of. Some were happy to leave America to return to the known frustrations of their former home. But most couldn't afford to leave, having spent their life savings to get here.

Since every settler family represented potential income to the railroads, they were reluctant to see their recruits fail. Eventually, the railroads learned that it worked better to ship immigrants by colonies, the theory being that a single family left on their own in the middle of nowhere may not adapt well, but a group of families with the same language and customs could give each other courage and strength. By the early 1880s, the Northern Pacific, the Santa Fe, and other transcontinental railroads were filling as many as fifty cars with immigrants and their belongings, all from the same area in Europe and all heading to the same destination in America.

The Moses of the Mennonites

Carl B. Schmidt was dubbed "Moses of the Mennonites" when, as an agent for the Santa Fe, he was sent to Europe to look for likely immigrants. He zeroed in on the German Mennonites living in Russia. Originally invited there in the eighteenth century by Catherine the Great in order to escape persecution in Germany, the Mennonites were promised freedom to build a German-speaking colony and remain exempt from military service, which is against their principles. In 1870, the Russian Czar took away their special privileges, declaring "One Czar, one religion, one language."

Schmidt entered Russia as a farm-machinery salesman and visited more than thirty villages, enticing them to America in their own language. He convinced them that Kansas plains were as good or better wheat lands than the Russian steppes, and in August 1874, thirty-four Mennonite families from the Russian Crimea arrived in Kansas. They had quietly converted their life savings into gold, which they used to purchase eight thousand acres of Santa Fe land. They built a colony of 150 A-frame houses along a graded main street and called it Gnadenau, or "Meadow of Grace."

Not long after, six hundred more Mennonites arrived, and in late September, another eleven hundred came. At first, Kansans were suspicious of the tall, bearded males and the woman in long, black dresses, but when word got out that they possessed two million dollars worth of gold, the Kansas governor himself held a reception for them.

In time, fifteen thousand Mennonites came to Kansas to create a wheat-growing paradise using their knowledge of dry land farming, which they learned on the arid Russian steppes. They even survived the droughts of 1879 and 1880 that caused many other farmers to abandon their land. They brought with them special wheat seed that was particularly tolerant of dry weather. They also improved the land with orchards, shade trees, and hedges.

They became known as such desirable immigrants that all manner of ploys were carried out by other railroads in order to attract them to their routes. Many promises were made, such as building them free windmills or irrigation systems, but since these promises were never in writing, they were rarely realized.

to America for groups such as criminals about to be released from prison and orphans.

For a long while, the relentless marketing of the U.S. was tolerated in these countries, until those governments realized that they were losing not only their surplus populations to the U.S., but also their most productive workers. Russia, for one, grew angry and threw an agent out of the country. Other countries simply waited for its citizens to return from America after discovering that life in this new "Eden" was not as easy and wonderful as promised.

The Cowboy Is Born

A good example of the interdependence that developed between East and West with the help of the railroad was the task of supplying the nation's meat in the years following the Civil War. A serious meat shortage in the North was threatening to cause problems feeding workers in that region's rapidly industrializing urban centers. In Texas, large cattle ranches were ready to supply the meat, but they needed a railroad to transport the animals. As yet, there was no east-west railroad along a southern route, and there was no rail connection between Texas and the transcontinental lines farther north. Enter the famous cattle drives depicted in Hollywood movies, and the birth of the western cowboy.

Cowboys were the men hired by Texas ranchers to drive the cattle to the nearest railroad connection, which at that time was the Kansas Pacific line in Missouri. All sorts of problems beset the cowboys as they drove their huge herds northward, the worst of which were farmers in Kansas who didn't want the herds trampling over their land and crops, and Indians defending their territory. Unable to get past these human obstacles, many cattle herds became caught in a pickle and died of starvation before they ever made it to the railroads.

Once the Kansas Pacific extended its track to Abilene, Kansas, however, things worked out much better for the cowboys. Abilene was farther West than the settled areas of Kansas, and the cowboys could follow the well-established Chisholm Trail (named for Jesse Chisholm, an early white trader with the Cherokee). The railroad launched a big advertising campaign for all ranchers in the South to get their stock to Abilene, and by the end of 1868, the railroad was scrambling to build enough holding pens and railroad cars to handle all the animals. The problem of meeting

Long cattle drives through the rough western landscape tested the strength of even the most rugged cowboys.

the demand for beef in the East was solved. Later, when the southern transcontinental lines were built, cross-country cattle drives became a thing of the past.

But the image of the cowboy lived on and has been a romantic symbol of the old West ever since. In truth, most observers of these cattle drivers, or Texans, at the time were not impressed with the skinny, dirty characters they encountered. One eastern magazine writer visiting the West expressed her lack of enthusiasm for the "rough man with shaggy hair and wild, staring eyes." The environment of the cowboy was also none too savory. Abilene, once the KP line was extended, quickly became a forty-saloon town in which cowboys could celebrate the end of a long cattle drive in a freewheeling and often vulgar way, with plenty of whiskey, gambling, dance-hall women, and taking the law into their own hands. Depraved as the reality was, in time the cowboy became a romanticized figure, immortalized in dime novels and Hollywood movies.

African-American cowboys

Nearly one-quarter of the cowboys taking part in the great cattle drives from Texas to railroad depots farther north were African-American. They served in almost every capacity, from the lowly wrangler up to the powerful cook, but the exalted position of trail boss or ranch foreman was forbidden them because of racial prejudice. The only exception to that rule was in the very rare case of an all-Black or Black-Mexican outfit. (Several African-American cowhands saved their wages to eventually buy their own spreads and thrive as independent ranchers, free of the limits set by racism.)

Most of the African-American cowboys were former slaves from Texas ranches; the rest came from the South and saw more promise for equality in the loosely structured West. Usually, they were disappointed. White cowboys were often quite prejudiced; but without the social institutions to reinforce racism, as in the South, Blacks could more easily prove themselves and earn acceptance. Three of the best-known Black cowboys, Nat Love, Jessie Stahl, and Bill Pickett (shown above) became popular rodeo performers, and Love's autobiography was widely read.

Mexican cowboys were also quite common, and American Indian cowboys as well, though by language and culture they were farther removed than African-Americans from the typical white cowboy. Naturally, once in the cattle towns, Black, Mexican, and Indian cowhands — as long as they had money to spend — were always welcome in the local saloons and brothels.

The Corporate Cowboys

If history has unjustly remembered the true cowboy as lawless, it has been too kind to a truly lawless sort of cowboy who had been active on the railroads from their inception. These were the men in charge of the railroad companies, the Stanfords, Durants, Huntingtons, and countless others, who fought only for their personal fortunes behind the facade of building railroads for the betterment of the country. In just the building of the first transcontinental line, the Big Four of the CP and Durant of the UP swallowed thirty-three million acres of public land, which they then sold to raise money for railroad construction. But in the scheme they slyly crafted, they pocketed millions of dollars through bogus contracts and then left the public with broke, barely functional railroad lines. The public paid for the transcontinental railroad over and over again through subsidies, loans, bond failures, and high freight rates.

The right side of the tracks

As the railroads created new towns out west, they also created new definitions of social classes. Depending on the direction the prevailing winds blew the black, sooty debris from the train engines, towns became divided into the "right" and "wrong" side of the tracks.

On the wrong side of the tracks, the poor lived in cheap-rent tenement housing, side by side with the noisy factories and mills, sleazy bars, and houses of ill repute. No one wanted to live there if he or she could avoid it. The right side of the tracks was reserved for the town's finest homes, churches, and expensive shops.

Railroad barons Jay Gould (below) and Jim Fisk (bottom) made millions manipulating Erie Railroad stock.

After building their part of the first transcontinental, the Big Four used their power and ill-gained fortunes to buy out all other lines in California, thereby creating a monopoly for themselves through which they continued to cheat Californians. They had built the Central Pacific for half of what the federal government paid them, pocketed the remainder, and then paid themselves millions of dollars in dividends from stock they acquired for nothing. In time, they controlled the state, buying up politicians and judges, forcing the public to pay interest on their own bonds, selling their land back to them at inflated prices, and taxing them through higher and higher freight rates.

For a long time, the general public believed wholeheartedly in the transcontinental railroad. They trusted the brave, heroic men building it for them, and they felt ownership in this grand effort. In time, the public snapped out of its reverie. One of the first big disappointments was the discovery that hundreds of miles of tracks and scores of bridges were so carelessly constructed during the "Great Race" that they would have to be destroyed and rebuilt— at the taxpayers' expense. Then, in 1873, the scandal of the UP-Credit Mobilier relationship was detailed in newspapers, letting the public in on the network of bribery and deception that had defined railroad business from the start.

The result of the disclosure was a sharp drop in UP stock, from one hundred dollars a share to fourteen dollars after the financial Panic of 1873. This opened the door for one of the most notorious of the Robber Barons to enter: Jay Gould. Gould, along with another Gilded Age pirate, Jim Fisk, had already made millions by gaining control of the Erie Railroad and then printing and selling bogus stock certificates and pocketing the proceeds. Gould and Fisk abandoned the railroad and left its stockholders without a penny of dividends while they walked away with millions. The western railroads were Gould's next victims. In 1873, he bought up one-third of Union Pacific stock, increased freight rates 133%, and manipulated the stock to a new high, whereupon he quietly sold out, taking perhaps $20 million with him. Later that decade, he bought up half of the Kansas Pacific line and played another trick with the stock so that he could sell his shares at an enormous profit. That's the way he operated.

And he was not alone. Several other slippery men manipulated railroad stock and dodged government investigations while they piled up vast fortunes. They convinced flimsy-spined congressional leaders that their actions were in the interest of the general public, but people everywhere were starting to see that greed was what really motivated them. But in that day, antimonopoly laws and stock-trading restrictions weren't around to prevent such skullduggery.

Regulation Takes Over

Since most politicians and government officials seemed unofficially on the payroll of the railroad barons, the people themselves — mostly midwestern farmers — took it upon themselves to fight the antics of these pirates. The farmers were frustrated. Two million new farms were producing more and more goods in the fertile West, and the eastern markets were becoming glutted with agricultural goods. The prices the farmers could expect for their goods began to go down, and with railroad freight rates remaining constant — or going up — the farmer's chance to make a profit disappeared. The farmers grouped together and turned on the railroads.

Through a farmers' organization originally intended for social and educational purposes — the National Grange of the Patrons of Husbandry — many farmers now sought political power. In 1875, more than twenty thousand local granges existed, representing eighty thousand members. By voting in blocs, the Grangers were able to get enough representatives into office to pass surprisingly tough laws establishing controls on freight rates. These were known as the Granger Laws of the 1870s.

But the railroad barons launched a vehement attack against the laws and the Grangers, whom they labeled communists. In 1876, the railroads brought the issue before the Supreme Court; the court upheld the Granger Laws. The railroad men responded with more attacks — subtle ones, like closing stations that hauled farmers' produce or lavishly backing Granger political opponents at election time. In 1886, the railroads brought another case to the Supreme Court, and this time the court reversed itself and ruled in favor of the railroads, saying that no state could regulate railroad commerce that passed beyond its limits. For the time being, the Grangers were defeated.

But the Supreme Court had also recommended that a federal agency be created to watch over the wily railroad corporations. A bill establishing the Interstate Commerce Commission was soon introduced in Congress, much to the dismay of the railroad barons. No matter how much they fought the bill, antirailroad sentiment had reached a fever pitch among the majority of Americans, and in 1887, the bill miraculously passed. At first, the five-man commission was only empowered to ensure that railroads not charge higher rates for short hauls than for long. The commission was not, as the farmers had hoped, allowed to set the maximum rates that railroads could charge. (That power was given the commission much later.) In any case, with this new law, the railroads became the first industry to be regulated by the federal government. The high-wheeling days of the robber barons were over.

Black farmers on the plains

After the U.S. Civil War, most African-Americans left plantation life to find jobs in the cities. But some responded to the call of cheap land on the plains and set out to establish themselves as farmers.

Many headed for Kansas, usually in large groups, and set up Black colonies; some were very successful, but most were short-lived. One, called Nicodemus, in northwest Kansas, got off to a bad start; but with perseverance and hard work, it did quite well. The families arrived too late in the fall of 1877 to plant crops, so they had no choice but to dig shelters in the hillsides and wait for spring. When spring came, they began breaking up the ground, but with only three horses among them, most of the work had to be done by hand with spades and hoes. Some plowing was done using a milk cow. In the first year, the settlers succeeded in planting several acres of corn per family. Things got easier with time, and by the autumn of 1880, the colony of eight hundred was thriving.

In contrast to third-class passengers — mostly immigrants and minorities who rode in overcrowded cars and sat on wooden benches — these passengers in first-class Pullman cars rode in perfect comfort, with upholstered seats and graciously decorated interiors.

CHAPTER FOUR

Riding the Rails

It would be hard for us to imagine today what train travel was like in the earlier days of the railroads. For the privileged, a train trip from Omaha, Nebraska, to Sacramento, California, in 1870, the first full year of operation on the transcontinental, was a romantic journey across a new and unknown terrain. First-class service meant warm and lovely car interiors, with thickly upholstered seats, nighttime entertainment, and fresh bed linens in a cozy sleeping berth. At first, most trains were not equipped to serve meals, so first-class passengers had to fill their stomachs along with all the other passengers during twenty-minute station stops in fairly simple depot restaurants. But if you could afford to spend just over one hundred dollars each way, you could ride on the *Pacific Hotel Express*, a lavishly decorated entertainment train that featured full-course meals to rival those served at the finest restaurants of the day.

Second-class passengers on the express trains, who paid eighty dollars for the full trip, were not offered comforts anywhere near those that greeted the first-class tourists. While the first-class cars were outfitted with plush, upholstered seats that converted into sleeping berths at night, second-class seats were crowded together, upholstered but upright only. They were not spoiled with steam heating, fresh linens, or all the fancy furnishings. They were not waited on by porters and conductors, nor were they entertained by organ players and singers. But they were not usually traveling the entire distance between Omaha and Sacramento anyway. Most second-class passengers were farmers, cowboys, miners, Native Americans, and the other folks that made up the population of the West. They were usually traveling short distances and didn't care about all the amenities.

For the passengers who traveled third class, especially members of ethnic minorities, such as African-Americans and Chinese, the reality of train travel was cold, dirty, and crowded cars with nothing but hard wooden benches. They paid forty dollars one way for a third-class fare reserved primarily for westward-bound immigrants looking to start a new life. And while the express trains guaranteed the trip in less than a week, the "Zulu cars," as they

The Chinese attempt to strike

The construction of the Central Pacific Railroad was accomplished mainly by Chinese workers, who were sometimes called Celestials because they referred to their homeland as the Celestial Kingdom. At work in the Sierras in 1867, they were described by one observer as "a great army laying siege to Nature in her strongest citadel. The rugged mountains look like stupendous ant-hills. They swarmed with Celestials, shoveling, wheeling, carting, drilling and blasting rocks and earth."

Receiving only thirty-one dollars per month while their white counterparts got forty-five dollars, five thousand Chinese walked out on strike, declaring, "Eight hours a day good for white men, all the same good for Chinamen." The company responded by offering to pay them thirty-five dollars, which they refused. One San Francisco newspaper, believing the strike to be part of a plot by Union Pacific managers to stall the progress of the Central Pacific, wrote an article insinuating that the fliers, written in Chinese and said to have started the strike, must have been part of a plot, because the Chinese had no capability to think for themselves and therefore the idea must have been put in their head by someone else.

Anxious to get work under way, the CP managers wired New York to see about getting ten thousand African-Americans to replace the Chinese. Deciding he wanted a faster resolution, Superintendent Crocker isolated the strikers and cut off their food supply. "I stopped the provisions on them," he said, "stopped the butchers from butchering, and used such coercive measures." His approach worked. Stuck in mountain camps and starving, the Chinese agreed to go back to work within a week.

were called, were frequently hitched to freight trains and given low priority on the tracks. For a trip that could take as many as ten sleepless nights, railroad travel for these passengers was not a romantic excursion, and the decision to go was not taken lightly.

Yet, in 1870, that first full year of operations for the transcontinental, plenty did go. Each day, one train left from each terminus and made the two-thousand-mile journey, usually in less than a week — a journey that had once taken up to six months. The majority of passengers were not traveling the whole line but were instead called "way" passengers, those with specific destinations along the way. In 1870, the ratio of way passengers to through passengers was five to four; by the early 1880s, that ratio grew to six to one. All totaled, 150,000 passengers rode on the CP-UP line in 1870, a number that swelled to almost a million by the mid-1880s.

With a couple of clever inventions, George Mortimer Pullman made millions building a virtual monopoly of specially outfitted passenger cars.

Pullman Defines Pleasure

First-class passengers on the transcontinental were mostly riding the trains for fun — *and* because one could scarcely call oneself worldly without having journeyed across the U.S. on the steam train. With the elite waiting to spend top dollar to board, the railroads catered to their every whim. That meant ultraluxury cars.

As early as 1864, industrialist and inventor George Mortimer Pullman had introduced two of his many innovations that would become lasting contributions to comfortable rail travel. The first was the hinged upper berth, upholstered and capable of being folded against the ceiling of the car. The second was the hinged seat and seatback that could be flattened into a bed of sorts. With these two relatively simple inventions, he created the first truly comfortable sleeping car. The long trip on the transcontinental became the perfect showcase for his revolutionary ideas in travel.

Pullman leased to the western railroads cars that were fully decorated and even staffed. Not only did he provide special sleeping cars, but his salon cars were appointed like the best drawing rooms in New York City. Rich upholstery and wall coverings, plus hand-carved, inlaid paneling made passengers feel as if they weren't even riding in a train. Add the elaborate meals prepared by Pullman chefs and served by Pullman waiters, with all the silver and linen provided in his exquisite dining cars, and passengers were treated like no less than royalty.

On a one-month special excursion trip between Cincinnati and San Francisco, dinners in the Pullman car consisted of blue-winged teal, antelope steaks, roast beef, boiled ham and tongue, broiled chicken, corn on the cob, fresh fruit, rolls, corn bread, and, in the Rocky Mountains, fresh trout. Engraved menus were sometimes presented, undoubtedly as much to put the passengers in an elegant frame of mind as to let them know what they would be eating.

For most rail passengers, however, meals were taken on the run at station restaurants while the train paused for fuel and water. Not unlike many people on the run today, passengers had twenty minutes or so to sit, order, and eat. Some of the so-called railroad eating houses were miserable, dust-ridden shanties with equally miserable food. That lasted until the late 1880s, when all express trains offered dining cars. These were nothing by comparison to the first-class Pullman cars. In the second-class dining cars, the same menu was offered over and over again, leading passengers like Susan Coolidge, a magazine journalist, to write: "It was necessary to look at one's watch to tell whether it was breakfast, dinner or supper, these meals presenting invariably the same salient features of beefsteak, fried eggs, fried potato."

Above: A 1905 Pullman compartment offered the finest in luxury travel.
Below: Until on-train dining cars were introduced in the 1880s, all passengers had to grab their meals on the run during twenty-minute station stops.

Service with a smile

To accommodate the passengers' every whim, Pullman hired and specially trained scores of railroad porters, most of whom were African-American. The first porter hired in 1867 is thought to have been a former slave, though not much is known about these men since they usually didn't leave any written documents. Some Mexican porters were hired for the southwestern railroads in later years.

All Pullman porters were trained in a side-tracked sleeping car in Chicago, where they learned how to make beds, care for linens, awake passengers, and handle luggage. Beginning porters gained experience as apprentices on regular trains and graduated to the longer western runs once they were pronounced ready. They were paid twenty to twenty-five dollars per month plus tips, a very meager salary when you consider that they had to pay for their uniforms and boot polish themselves.

At some point, all porters were given the nickname "George," probably after their boss, George Pullman, in a rather humiliating reminder of their subservience and anonymity.

Fred Harvey's Civilizing Influence

The Fred Harvey Company's well-trained young waitresses, known as "The Harvey Girls," had a dramatic effect on train-stop dining – and society – in the West. They provided great restaurant service as well as a civilizing influence on western men.

Such gastronomical limitations were overcome, at least on the Atchison, Topeka & Santa Fe Railroad, when Fred Harvey arrived on the scene. He was himself an English immigrant and found great success in the States when he developed his depot restaurant chain, employing good food and good service with the help of his "Harvey Girls." He started as manager of the restaurant at the Topeka station in a building rented from the railroad, and his efforts revolutionized railroad dining. His restaurants became the rave of the nation. So efficient was Harvey House service that the restaurant even had conductors taking passengers' orders as the train approached and telegraphing the choices so passengers could sit down to a hot plate immediately upon arrival. The same formula worked all along the line, until he had built a chain of forty-seven depot restaurants and diners, fifteen railroad hotels, and thirty dining cars. Thanks to Harvey, the Santa Fe became famous for fine food and service.

But that's not all. The line also became famous for its civilizing influence on the otherwise rowdy West. For waitresses, Harvey employed only "young women of good character, attractive and intelligent," eighteen to thirty years of age, at a monthly salary of $17.50, plus tips and room and board. The women lived in a Harvey dormitory with a chaperoned courting parlor and a 10:00 P.M. curfew. The advertisement may as well have read "suitable and ready for marriage," since the respectable women, a new breed in the dance-hall West, were

Railside Indian craft shows

In addition to his culinary successes as railside dining magnate, Fred Harvey also sought to magnify his wealth by catering to the tourist fascination with Native American life and culture. He cut a deal with his Santa Fe Railroad buddies to set up shops and demonstrations highlighting Indian crafts and customs in an effort to boost ridership on the Santa Fe Railroad.

The Harvey Company's Indian Department opened its first showrooms in 1901 in prime tourist locations, such as the south rim of the Grand Canyon and the Alvarado Hotel adjacent to the railroad depot in Albuquerque, New Mexico. Outside the buildings, Indians sold pottery and jewelry to passersby, while inside, Harvey had recreated Navajo and Pueblo villages and hired weavers and silversmiths to demonstrate their skills.

The Indians were required to be on duty whenever trains were scheduled to arrive, which meant early morning and sometimes evening hours. The manager of the Indian Department, Herman Schweizer, once complained of tardiness on the part of the Native Americans and revealed his capitalistic attitude toward the showroom, saying, "I like to see my factory in full blast." Schweizer treated the Indian artists with a cavalier attitude when it came to the price and design of merchandise purchased from them. In several letters, he tells the Indians exactly what colors to use and not use and what size to make the rugs to make them appealing to white tourists. He wanted to cash in on the current fashion of Southwest-style interior decorating, and he exploited the talents of Native Americans in order to do so.

Southwestern Native American items were not the only commodities collected and sold in the Harvey showrooms. A 1905 photograph of the Albuquerque salesroom shows southwestern baskets and textiles, Samoan tapa cloth, Maori carvings from New Zealand, Zulu shields, a Chilkat blanket, and an Inuit kayak.

courted and married by more than five thousand western men. (Harvey lost so many good employees that he eventually added a clause to their contracts requiring them to forfeit half their wages if they married before the end of the first year.) A 1944 Hollywood musical called "The Harvey Girls," starring Judy Garland, depicts the fragile truce between the "bad" saloon girls and the "good" Harvey girls in a western town. And since those legions of "bad" boys usually *married* the latter, Harvey was thus dubbed the "Civilizer of the West."

The Zulu Cars

The cheapest and most uncomfortable way to travel west was on the third- and lowest-class cars, which became known as the Zulu cars. These cars were reserved primarily for immigrants, who were herded on more like baggage than humans. The design varied from railroad to railroad, but for the most part, Zulu cars consisted of wooden benches, at first without backs, so that people had to sleep on the floor underneath them or in the aisles. At one end of the car a curtained-off area provided the only communal latrine; at the other end a single coal-burning stove provided the only heat (when necessary). Cooking stoves were added in the late 1880s so the immigrants could at least cook their own food, but they turned out to be more of a fire hazard than a convenience in the all-wood cars.

Eventually, a sort of Zulu sleeping car was designed, with two boxlike benches that wood planks could be placed across to form beds. A second level of bare-planked berths was installed above. Upholstery was never used in the Zulu cars, and conductors on the railroads made extra money from these passengers by selling them wood planks and crudely made cushions for a couple of dollars worth of extra comfort.

"Separate but equal" cars for Blacks

Segregation in the South was a way of life, but in progressive New Orleans, African-Americans enjoyed more rights and privileges than in most southern cities. In the years following the Civil War, segregation of street cars ended, Black voter registration began, schools were integrated on an experimental basis, and interracial marriage was made legal. The city also elected the nation's first African-American mayor and sent hundreds of Blacks to state and federal legislatures.

But by 1890, the rights of African-Americans were being chipped away by the vigilant efforts of white supremacists, and segregation reappeared when the Louisiana Separate Car Act went into effect. The law required state railroads to provide "equal but separate" railroad cars for white and Black travelers, no matter if just one Black person wished to travel and a white car was still half empty.

To challenge this law, a coalition of African-Americans in 1892 planted a fair-skinned Black man, Homer Plessy, on a whites-only car and welcomed the legal battle that followed. The plan backfired, however, because the tides of racism were turning at that moment in Louisiana history. Judge after judge sided with the law segregating the races, and the case continued all the way to the Supreme Court. The famous 1896 case, *Plessy v. Ferguson,* is hailed as the unjust but necessary precursor to the even more famous 1954 decision, *Brown v. the Board of Education,* which threw out the "separate but equal" approach to segregation on the grounds that it violated the Fourteenth Amendment Rights of Blacks.

The interiors of "Zulu cars" were quite different from first-class accommodations. Immigrants were packed together for weeks of travel with one stove at each end of the car as the only source of heat.

Passengers were usually separated by sex on the Zulu cars, and sometimes by race. The purpose of the former can only be guessed at, but according to one male account, it was a blessing to be spared the crying and general loudness of babies and young children, who naturally stayed with their mothers. Separation by race seems only to have happened in the case of large groups of Chinese or African-American travelers, presumably to avoid any interracial conflict. Racism was alive and well in America.

The Immigrant's Experience

In 1879, Scottish writer Robert Louis Stevenson, at age twenty-nine (before he became famous for *Dr. Jekyll and Mr. Hyde* and *Treasure Island*), traveled to America and rode the transcontinental in an immigrant car, documenting his none-too-pleasant experience. His misery began at the New York immigrant reception center, the one with the deceptively romantic name of "Castle Garden." Here immigrants were sorted, documented, and then sent to the offices of various railroad agents, depending on their destination. What was intended to be an orderly clearinghouse for thousands of new arrivals was not in the slightest bit hospitable, according to Stevenson. "It was plain that the whole system, if system there was, had utterly broken down," he wrote. He was eventually directed to a large waiting shed: "It was dark, the wind blew clean through it from end to end, and here I found a great block of passengers and baggage, hundreds of one and tons of the other. . . . I may say we stood like sheep, and that the porters charged among us like so many maddened sheep dogs; and I believe these men were no longer answerable for their acts."

When he had finally been directed to the proper railway station, "There was no waiting room, no refreshment room; the cars were locked; and for at least another hour, or so it seemed, we had to camp upon the draughty, gas-lit platform. I sat on my valise, too crushed to observe my neighbors; but as they were all cold, and wet, and weary, and driven stupidly crazy by the mismanagement to which we had been subjected, I believe they can have been no happier than myself." Finally, they were loaded onto the train to Council Bluffs, Iowa, there to be transferred to the Union Pacific and on to San Francisco. Not having been advised to color his wrists with a stinging solution of mercury, he was already covered with the itchy, open sores of disease that frequently spread among passengers on the vermin-infested, third-class railcars.

In Council Bluffs, Stevenson treated himself to one night of relative luxury, opting to pay the higher price at a Union Pacific hotel rather than spend the night in the local Emigrant House, a large dormitory provided by the railroad. The next morning, hundreds of immigrants waited to be loaded onto the train west. A railroad official called the name of each passenger or family, who picked up their bundles and boarded the rearmost car. Zulu cars were always loaded first, and immigrants routinely waited several hours cramped in their cars while the rest of the train was loaded. Stevenson grew frustrated as twenty baggage cars were attached to his car, with plenty of bumping and jarring, in a procedure that took almost half the day. During the journey, the mixed-freight train on which he traveled spent hours stalled on sidetracks, waiting for the express trains to pass by.

For ten nights, Stevenson slept on a bed of planks with three straw cushions he had purchased from the conductor for $2.50. With two fellow travelers, he shared the improvised bunk as well as the cookware, food, and toiletries they were able to afford only by pooling their money. The train conductor advised passengers to "chum together" to buy the bedding from him; other goods were purchased from the train's "news butcher," including coffee, sugar, hand towels, soap, and even books. Breakfast could be bought from the farmers' wives who boarded the train at the first local station and sold fresh milk, eggs, and cakes. "Soon from end to end the car would be filled with little parties breakfasting upon the bed boards. It was the pleasantest hour of the day," Stevenson wrote.

Lunch and dinner were eaten in depot restaurants at special immigrant prices. The stops were usually for no more than twenty minutes, so if a passenger hadn't been served yet or hadn't had time to finish his or her meal when the whistle blew, tough luck. Stevenson complained that it seemed the conductors on immigrant trains got a perverse pleasure from pulling out of the stations without even an "All aboard!" or a whistle toot as warning; it was a practice that sent passengers running and scrambling to get back on the train.

Because he was ill during most of his journey, Stevenson spent little time thinking of anything other than the miseries of his immediate surroundings.

Characters of the western trains

Though the train cars themselves carefully separated the wealthy from the poor, the whites from all others, the railroad stations were the mixmasters of the West. When the trains stopped, everyone was forced to mingle on the platform. Here, whites curiously considered the Indians they caught glimpses of, even going so far as to give money to Indian women for the chance to look at their papooses. Easterners also enjoyed viewing the western characters they'd read so much about in newspapers and popular novels. Seeing men with knives and revolvers strapped to their waists and boots gave them a thrill. A parson from London wrote: "It was curious to see a rough-booted, broad-brimmed fellow strutting up and down the train with his revolver slung behind him like a short blunt tail. But, of course, if you leave them alone they don't meddle with you. They only shoot their friends and acquaintances as a rule."

Foreigners on trains were often disgusted by the American habits of chewing tobacco and drinking whiskey. Brass cuspidors lined the walls of the trains, and some made a game out of spitting accurately into them, while others roamed the trains occasionally saying to new acquaintances, "Smile?," which was western slang for "Have a sip of whiskey?" Poker-faced professional gamblers, bedecked in fine clothes and gold jewelry, were also common on these trains, ready to trick unsuspecting travelers out of their money. Add to this picture the scores of immigrants from all parts of the world. Indeed, people-watching must have been a great pastime in the early years of the transcontinental railroads.

But when he did watch the passing countryside, he was none too impressed: "At sea on the plains of Nebraska, I made my observatory on the top of a fruit-waggon, and sat by the hour upon that perch to spy about me, and to spy in vain for something new. It was a world almost without feature; an empty sky; front and back, the line of the railway stretched from horizon to horizon. On either hand, the green plain ran till it touched the skirts of heaven. The train toiled over this infinity like a snail." When he did find a small town, in the form of several clustered houses, he wrote, "The mind is loath to accept it for a piece of reality; and it seems incredible that life can go on with so few properties, or that the great child, man, finds entertainment in so bare a playroom."

Other Train Terrors

While Stevenson suffered the routine discomforts of immigrant-class travel, he at least arrived in California without experiencing the other likely terrors of a transcontinental journey. Train bandits, buffalo stampedes, washed-out bridges, derailments, crashes, prairie fires, dangerous weather, and attacks by Indians seeking justice for lands, lives, and culture lost to encroachment by European-Americans — all were possibilities. Wealthier passengers viewing the West as tourists — not settlers — usually hoped to see one or all of these on their trip, particularly Indians and buffalo, for the sake of amusement. Most were disappointed; Indians were scarce, and buffalo populations had already been decimated.

Train robbers, on the other hand, were having a heyday in the 1870s. Just a year and a half after the transcontinental was completed, the first heist was carried out by a gang of six robbers who boarded the eastbound Central Pacific. At 1:30 A.M., as the train stopped in Truckee, California, they surprised the engineer and fireman and held them at gunpoint while they disengaged the rest of the train, except for the express car, where gold, silver,

Opposite page: Top: Train robbers found ideal victims in unsuspecting, captive travelers. *Middle:* Fascinated by the romance and danger of train travel, the American public devoured publications with railroad adventure stories. *Bottom:* The bandit Sam Bass — immortalized in song and legend — robbed many trains before he was killed by a Texas cop in 1878, at age twenty-seven.

and money were kept. They made off with forty thousand dollars — a huge amount in those days. After they had gone, the engineer reversed the engine nine miles back to where it had been uncoupled from the others. Neither the conductor nor the passengers had any idea of what had taken place. Ridiculously, the same train was looted again less than twenty-four hours later, near Toana, Nevada. Those bandits got away with almost as much as the first.

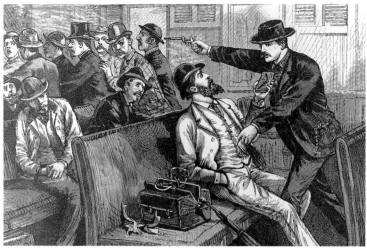

One of the most feared and famous train bandits was Jesse James, who first robbed a Rock Island Line train in 1873. During this first robbery, James and his gang derailed the train by loosening a rail, tying a rope to it, and pulling on it once the train came into view. The train plunged over onto its side, killing the engineer instantly, and a number of passengers were injured. While some of his men took money from the safe in the express car, others went through the train and at gunpoint relieved the passengers of their cash and jewels.

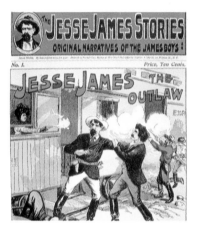

Another train thief immortalized in song and legend was Sam Bass of Indiana. To finance his lifestyle of expensive racehorses, women, and booze, he first robbed stagecoaches in the Black Hills, then moved up to trains. In 1877, he and a gang of five started with a Union Pacific train in Nebraska, unloading the express car of sixty thousand dollars — a record for train robberies. He followed that with robberies on the Houston & Texas Central and the Texas & Pacific, but he never found that kind of loot again; for his efforts on one heist, he got only fifty-two dollars. He was eventually killed by a Texas Ranger when he was just twenty-seven. But he was remembered because of rumors that he buried stashes of loot in unlikely places; fifty years after his death, people with maps and tips were still trying to locate his supposed treasure — unsuccessfully.

The biggest threat to passenger safety was train wrecks, which happened frequently enough to raise public demands for better railroad management. Many such wrecks happened because of bad communication about which trains were using what lines. The majority of those problems were solved by 1870, when most lines had warning signal devices and telegraph capabilities. But plenty of other wrecks were caused by bridges giving out, as was the case on August 10, 1887, when two engines pulling fifteen cars of tourists on the Toledo, Peoria & Western Railroad line headed toward Niagara Falls, New York. The train rolled onto a bridge, and after the first locomotive made it across, the bridge collapsed under the second, and all fifteen cars plunged down the canyon.

Eighty-four people were drowned or burned alive in that disaster.

In the West, trains encountering trestle bridges weakened by spring thaws often required their passengers to disembark and walk their way across the bridge, tie by tie, with one eye on the raging river far below. Meanwhile, the engine and expendable freight cars would be sent across to test the strength of the bridge, to be followed by the passenger cars if all was okay. Then the train was recoupled and could resume. Once in a while, a passenger might fall to his or her death while walking over the bridge.

Derailments not caused by anything other than poorly laid track also occurred with disturbing regularity, especially in the early transcontinental days as a result of hasty track construction during the Great Race. Often, some loss of life would result; or, at the very least, passengers would be tossed and tumbled a bit as the cars bounced along the tracks.

Running the Rails

Railroading was the great adventure of the century, and many kids grew up knowing just what they wanted to be — a railroad engineer. Their first

Railroad work was often life threatening. *Above:* Train wrecks such as this Illinois Railroad scene occurred when bridges washed out, track was damaged, communications failed, or thieves planned an ambush. *Opposite page:* A man is trapped under the engine (above), while (below) a train brakeman jumps along car roofs on a moving train to apply each brake, regardless of the weather.

Fun turned tragic

The American public had a peculiar fascination with train wrecks, so much so that at the instigation of a ticket agent named William George Crush, the Missouri, Kansas & Texas Railroad agreed to stage a collision between two locomotives and charge people a fee to watch. The scheme was intended as a publicity stunt for the railroad and to make money. It was advertised in newspapers and on posters for months in advance.

The incident took place on September 15, 1896, near Waco, Texas. Between thirty thousand and forty thousand people were assembled, and a battalion of sheriff's deputies were on hand to keep the crowd a safe distance away. The two engines — one painted green, the other red — backed up a mile and came at each other full throttle, each trailing six empty passenger cars behind them. At sixty miles per hour, they slammed into each other, exploding in a burst of hot metal, splintered wood, and boiling water that traveled much farther than was expected. Two people died and scores were injured, including a photographer who lost an eye but continued taking pictures of the melee that ensued.

impressions of the great Iron Horses — all shiny and brass, with whistles blowing, heading for destinations spanning the continent — downplayed the realities of working on the railroad. More realistic accounts from Henry Clay French and J. Harvey Reed, two men who spent their lives on the railroad and documented much of what they lived, testify to the crazy hours, the homelessness, and the hazards they encountered.

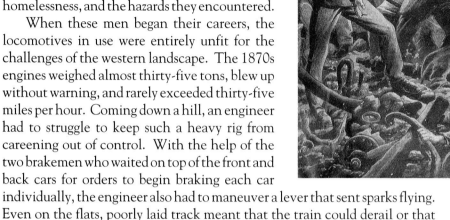

When these men began their careers, the locomotives in use were entirely unfit for the challenges of the western landscape. The 1870s engines weighed almost thirty-five tons, blew up without warning, and rarely exceeded thirty-five miles per hour. Coming down a hill, an engineer had to struggle to keep such a heavy rig from careening out of control. With the help of the two brakemen who waited on top of the front and back cars for orders to begin braking each car individually, the engineer also had to maneuver a lever that sent sparks flying. Even on the flats, poorly laid track meant that the train could derail or that a trestle bridge might collapse and there was nothing even the finest engineer could do about it.

In 1888, the first year statistics were kept, 2,070 railroad men were killed on the job and 20,148 were injured. Most likely to be killed in action were engineers, firemen, "brakies" (who had to jump from roof to roof on a moving train to apply brakes, even in bad weather), and switchmen (the men in the railyards who fastened the hook and pin that connected one car to another). For engineers and firemen, the two in the engine cab, the trick to staying alive was in knowing just when to bail out before an unavoidable wreck. Brakies were often killed by falling from the trains as they jumped from car to car. And no matter how good a switchman was at judging time and distance as he jumped between coupling cars, eventually his luck ran out, and if he didn't lose his life by being squashed between cars, he at least lost a few fingers or a limb. In 1893, about the time French and Reed retired, reliable air brakes and automatic couplers were required by law and saved countless lives.

Still, the men who worked for the railroads wouldn't have traded their dangerous existence for anything in the world. Most railroad engineers worked their way up from the very bottom of the ladder. They started as yardboys and messengers, then became switchmen or brakemen or firemen, and eventually proved themselves capable of commanding their own engine. They gave the best years of their lives to the railroad and were at the beck and call of the railroad schedule, which made it very difficult to have a normal family life. As a result, the railroad crews became their family. Even their off-duty hours were spent together in the bands, baseball teams, and volunteer firefighting groups they organized. There was a strong sense of loyalty and unity among railroaders.

For such a dangerous job, railroad engineers earned sixty dollars per month, provided they logged at least twenty-five hundred miles that month. Pay was deducted from their salary if they didn't meet that minimum, but nothing more was given them for extra miles. For the firemen's backbreaking labor of keeping the engine fed with coal, he earned about two dollars a day, or forty dollars per month. All the other men earned less than the engineer and fireman. For all the dangers and demands of their jobs, nobody working on the railroad was paid very well.

A financial depression in the late 1870s made the situation worse. The B & O Railroad was the first line to cut back the wages of its workers, making it almost impossible for a hardworking man to support his family, while at the same time the men who owned the railroad added to their millions. The result was the first railroad workers' strike. It started in Martinsburg, West Virginia, when workers seized railroad property and held up service, refusing to give up until their wages were restored. In the following days, strikes spread to every railroad line, and the country's rail system was at a standstill.

In response, President Rutherford B. Hayes sent federal troops to Martinsburg to break the strike, but what followed was a battle between the workers

The 1894 railroad strike that started in Chicago ended when National Guard troops fired into crowds of protesting workers. Many strikers died, yet workers' calls for improved working conditions were ignored. Nonetheless, their fight showed the government that workers' complaints and their new labor unions would have to be taken seriously.

and troops. Several workers were shot, and lots of railroad property was damaged. Troops were also sent to Pittsburgh, where strikers had stalled the Pennsylvania Railroad. In the clash there, twenty-six people were killed. Much of the city was destroyed when angry citizens came to the aid of the railroad workers. In other large cities from Boston to San Francisco, outraged citizens demonstrated against the killing of fellow citizens by the nation's own troops and against the greed of the railroad owners in general.

Eugene V. Debs, one of the first men to stand up for the rights of railway workers, helped found the American Railway Union. He was jailed for his role in starting the 1894 strike.

In two weeks, the whole strike was over. More than one hundred people were dead, thousands more were injured, and the strikers returned to work for their original pay or less. Some lost their jobs altogether as punishment for striking. The railroad owners, in order to prevent future strikes and damage to property, formed private armies to protect themselves and their trains. Out of all this came a new attitude among workers about how they should be treated, and they began to form labor unions to defend themselves politically. The four railway labor unions were the Brotherhood of Locomotive Engineers, the Brotherhood of Locomotive Firemen, the Brotherhood of Railroad Trainmen, and the Brotherhood of Sleeping Car Porters (the country's first Black union).

Another bad depression in 1893 brought a man named Eugene V. Debs, a billing clerk for the Brotherhood of Locomotive Firemen, into the spotlight as a labor organizer. He was moved by the plight of the average worker and helped start the American Railway Union in an effort to unite all railroad workers (except Blacks, who were excluded by a vote of 112 to 100) in order to fight for better working conditions. In 1894, another huge strike shook the country. This time it was against the Pullman Palace Car Company in Chicago, again for distributing stock dividends to rich owners while cutting worker wages. In protest, passenger trains across the country were stalled, and hundreds of cars in the Chicago yards were burned. Troops were brought in, and again people died. Debs was arrested and, in jail, began his career as a Socialist, believing that socialism was the only form of government that cared enough for the average worker.

Nothing tangible changed in the railroad worker's life immediately following the Pullman strike either, but it at least showed the federal government that the working class was deadly serious about being respected by management. Labor unions of all kinds gained a great deal of momentum during this period and would soon become a powerful force that government would have to work with in the future.

Thousands of African-American sleeping-car porters were hired by the Pullman Palace Car Company of Chicago to cater to every whim of mostly white travelers.

CHAPTER FIVE

Railroads in the Twentieth Century

After the Civil War, African-Americans in ever-increasing numbers left the South and headed north, where they believed they could find better jobs and leave the emotional scars of slavery behind. Indeed, the more industrial North was in desperate need of huge numbers of laborers, no matter what their color, as long as they could do the job. Other companies were very specific in the type of work they offered African-Americans. One such company, while offering bona fide jobs to Blacks, also kept them in a form of servitude to whites.

The first Black Pullman porter was hired in the 1850s. By 1893, the Pullman Palace Car Company in Chicago was the country's largest employer of Black labor, with nearly twenty thousand African-Americans on the payroll. That year, President Grover Cleveland publicly commended Pullman at the World's Fair in Chicago for his good work in hiring African-Americans in jobs of "service." It is no coincidence that for nearly a century, all Pullman porters were Black. While they were grateful for the chance to make an honest living and build families and communities of their own, the porters were in many ways still slaves. For decades, they accepted the situation, as long as they had their freedom and pride; but as the Golden Age of the Railroads was in full swing, they formed the nation's first Black union and joined their voice to the din of protest rising from the nation's class of exploited workers.

An explosion of growth in the nation's rail system during the 1870s and 1880s meant that there were more and more trains, most of them equipped with Pullman sleeping cars. After the first transcontinental was built, several different routes followed. The southern route was finished in 1881; a route connecting St. Paul, Minnesota, with the Pacific Northwest was completed two years later. Chicago and California were linked by direct service shortly afterwards. In just those two decades, 110,675 miles were added to the system.

By 1916 — the peak of U.S. railroad transportation — a grand total of 254,000 miles of track were in constant use. After 1916, improvements in railroad technology and more direct routing meant that less track was

The African-American exodus to the North

In the early 1900s, many African-Americans in the South realized that the Civil War had done little to change the attitudes and behavior of southern whites. There would still be plenty of racism and not much real opportunity for freed slaves to be financially independent. Most found themselves getting further into debt as tenant farmers on the same plantations where they had been slaves.

Seeking good jobs and true freedom, tens of thousands of Blacks left for the cities of the North. This early migration helps explain why cities like Chicago, New York, and Detroit have large African-American populations today.

As described in the lines of this poem of the day, these refugees used whatever means they could to migrate north, but the railroad was the transportation of choice:

> Some are coming on the passenger,
> Some are coming on the freight.
> Others will be found walking,
> For none have time to wait.

Reflecting a growing sense of concern over the South's reduced African-American population (and cheap labor pool), one newspaper in Georgia sounded the alarm over the exodus in the following terms: "Everybody seems to be asleep about what is going on right under their noses. That is, everybody except those farmers who have awakened up of mornings recently to find every male Negro over 21 . . . gone — to Cleveland, to Pittsburgh, to Chicago. . . ."

While alarm over the reduction of the South's Black population (and cheap labor pool) was probably common, no doubt the hearts of African-Americans making the exodus were filled with a sense of hope and anticipation:

> I've watched the trains as they disappeared
> Behind the clouds of smoke,
> Carrying the crowds of working men
> To the land of hope.

necessary for efficient service. At the same time, the automobile had been invented and was winning the hearts of Americans. More and more roads and highways were built. By 1945 and the end of the World War II, the system of tracks was reduced to its present size of about 150,000 miles.

The Life of a Pullman Porter

At first, the Pullman porters approached their jobs with abundant cheer and energy. "Good morning, Ma'am," "Good evening, Mr. Smith," and other pleasantries were expressed with a wide smile as mostly white railroad passengers boarded the fancy Pullman cars. They were proud to be porters, proud that they could travel the country and see things their friends and neighbors could only imagine. They learned the rules of the Pullman school with precision, including twelve-step directions on how to serve a beer to a customer and pages on how to make a bed properly.

The porters did their job so well that the public came to expect that they would do anything for a tip, and with a smile. Some passengers humiliated porters just to see how far they were willing to go. They might dangle tips in front of a porter while demanding that he bark like a dog or let their children ride him like a horse. If he refused, he lost the tip — and that might not be all. As angry as a porter might be inside, he had no way of refusing what was asked of him without risking his job.

The Pullman Company had written volumes of very specific rules dictating a porter's behavior in every situation. Many of these rules reveal just how subservient the porters were forced to be. A porter was *required* to smile and formally greet passengers. When a white woman wished to board a car, the white train conductor should help her; only in his absence was a Black porter allowed to assist her, and then *only* if she requested help. Most importantly, a porter could never disagree with a passenger; no matter the situation, the passenger was *always* right. This sometimes led to situations where Pullman porters were teased and harassed by aggressive groups of white travelers. Still, porters had no right to defend themselves, not on a Pullman train.

A Pullman porter had to follow exactly the rules of service that dictated his every move. For example, he could never help a white woman off the train unless the white conductor was unable to help her and only if she asked for help.

Porters were paid meagerly — on purpose, some say, so that they would work harder for tips to round out their salaries. They were also responsible for any ashtrays, linens, or other railroad property that might disappear from their cars. (Passengers often helped themselves to souvenirs, so this happened quite often.) Replacements were deducted from their salaries. If a porter tried to protect his salary by "suggesting" that a passenger might have packed something by mistake, the passenger might become upset and the porter would instantly lose his job. It was a no-win situation. Porters even had to supply their own equipment and polish for shining passengers' shoes. With these rules, most porters could hardly support their families on what they took home each month. Other Pullman pol-

icies dictated how many hours per week a porter had to work, and how much sleep he could have each night of a cross-country train trip — three hours of sleep on the first night out, none on the following, and so on. Yet, if a porter was caught sleeping on the job, he was instantly dismissed.

In order to survive, the porters relied heavily on each other for support and humor to keep them going. They told endless stories amongst themselves, sometimes in a code language they developed to avoid being reported by spies that were often planted by management. It was an enormously difficult way of life, but the majority of porters were loyal to the company nonetheless, just thankful for a regular job and income.

The First Black Union

Fighting for better conditions through labor unions wasn't an option for porters before the turn of the century. When Eugene Debs organized white Pullman workers in the American Railway Union (ARU), Blacks were not invited to join. In the 1894 strike against the Pullman Company, ARU members representing 90 percent of the company workforce walked off their jobs. Pullman fired all the rest, who were Black. When the strike was over, the workers were rehired, but only after they signed an agreement never to

---

"The most dangerous Negro in America": Asa Philip Randolph, 1889-1979

In 1911, a young African-American named Randolph left the South and arrived in New York's Harlem, which was already home to more than sixty thousand Blacks. He put himself through City College working several unskilled jobs, the memories of which served him well as he set out on a lifelong career of speaking out for better treatment of his fellow African-Americans.

In 1917, Randolph and a friend started a politically radical Black magazine called *The Messenger*. His ardent, socialist opinions about the exploitation of Black labor by white bosses were published in the magazine. When World War I started, mainstream African-American leaders were calling on their brethren to join forces with whites to fight; Randolph wanted to know why Blacks should cooperate with men who "thought of them as animals without rights." For that he earned the label by some whites as "the most dangerous Negro in America."

At the same time, a group of Pullman sleeping-car porters were trying to organize a union, but they needed a leader from outside their ranks because any Pullman employee caught talking union was immediately fired. They chose Randolph as the man to lead them in their battle. At first, he refused, choosing instead to use his magazine to gather support for their cause. But the men eventually pressured him into accepting the role. In 1925, he launched the Brotherhood of Pullman Sleeping Car Porters with an initial membership of two hundred men.

Randolph traveled the nation setting up local offices and recruiting new members. (He was able to spend all his time in this cause largely because his wife ran a successful hairdressing salon in Harlem.) It wasn't easy. The Pullman Company tried to sabotage the union in its early years by offering just enough to keep most porters loyal to the company. Pullman managers fired anyone connected to the union, no questions asked, so many porters were afraid to join for fear of losing their jobs. But Randolph succeeded in convincing many porters that they had a right to demand a better life, and membership drives across the country brought membership in 1928 to an all-time high of seven thousand. Randolph devoted his best years and his reputation to the twelve-year struggle to have the Brotherhood recognized by the Pullman Company. Finally, in 1937, the Pullman Company agreed to negotiate with union officials for better working conditions for the porters, thanks in large part to Randolph's perseverance.

The Brotherhood was the largest union of Black workers in America and the first Black union to negotiate a contract with a major corporation.

---

join a union while working for Pullman. The Blacks were also forced to sign. Though they were never respected enough to be included in early attempts by labor to organize, they were affected by the union's actions.

When a new generation of Pullman porters talked of organizing in the 1920s, older porters declined to join them. They felt the company treated them well enough. Also, Pullman managers had made it crystal clear that

anyone known to be connected with any union would be fired immediately. Dozens of porters were fired on the spot as soon as they were suspected of union activity, no matter how many years they had worked for the company.

For a century, African-American porters served on Pullman cars. The Pullman Company's reputation was in large part made by these "Ambassadors of Hospitality," as they were called. And for seventy years, the porters uncomplainingly played the role designed for them. It wasn't until 1925 that African-American porters felt mistreated enough to form the nation's first all-Black union, the Brotherhood of Sleeping Car Porters. After a long battle, the Pullman Company reluctantly recognized it and negotiated new working terms with its leaders.

An Era of Unabashed Luxury

With the signature Pullman porters standing by with a smile, the fortunes of the Pullman Palace Car Company grew and grew. Although other companies, including the railroad companies themselves, went into the business of designing and operating sleeping cars, no one could keep up with the Pullman company. One by one, Pullman bought out all the smaller companies, and in 1899, he swallowed his largest rival, the Wagner Palace Car Company, so that by 1927 he had a true monopoly of the sleeping-car business.

From 1880 to 1927, Pullman's cars reached new pinnacles of comfort and design. His parlor cars frequently housed pianos and organs to entertain the travelers; some had well-stocked libraries with plush, upholstered reading chairs. The really fancy cars had a separate lounge for women, where afternoon tea was served them, and a club car for men, where they could drink, smoke, and chew tobacco without offending the women. (In 1919, Prohibition made the manufacturing and use of alcohol illegal, thus putting an end to the need for cars in which men could drink. The ultimate death blow to gender-segregated cars came when "Flappers" — those fashionable women of the 1920s — took up social smoking and put

Above: The Brotherhood of Sleeping Car Porters, organized in 1925, was the first successful African-American labor union. *Below:* Fashionable 1920s women known as "Flappers" (because they flapped, or tossed aside, social conventions) helped narrow the gap between the sexes by smoking in public. Now, separate cars for men to smoke away from women were no longer necessary.

Mexicans working on the railroads

Mexicans were important to railroad construction, especially in California and the Southwest. During the 1880s, the crews laying track for the Texas and Mexican Railroad were predominantly Mexican. A newspaper in Arizona wrote: "It is difficult to get white men to work, the wages being only $1.50 a day, and board $5 per week with some minor changes, which reduce a man's net earnings." The company's solution was to recruit Mexicans.

In 1894, Mexicans were brought to Santa Barbara, California, to work on the Southern Pacific line. The "Chinese section hands" were replaced by "a gang of Mexicans," wrote one local paper. By 1900, the Southern Pacific Railroad had nearly five thousand Mexican workers in California.

The Atchison, Topeka and Santa Fe also hired thousands of Mexicans, especially for work on its rails in the Southwest. During the labor shortages that occurred with World War II, the Santa Fe hired seven thousand Mexican nationals (16 percent of the whole workforce) to help keep up with the surge in rail travel during the war years.

an end once and for all to the notion that women should be offended by cigarette smoke.)

At the close of the nineteenth century, the fanciest train ever to adorn tracks (up to that time) was introduced. The *Pennsylvania Limited* set new standards of luxury travel, along with a few practical improvements. Passengers could now travel freely and safely between cars, not having to risk life and limb in open air by jumping over the couplers, but by passing through vestibules to get from car to car. Also, electricity was used for the first time to light the cars, significantly reducing the risk of fire ignited by gas or kerosene lamps. From a decorative standpoint, the train also set new standards of artistry and comfort. Car exteriors were elaborately painted in green, cream, and red. Inside, the private drawing rooms and sleeping compartments were finished with a variety of expensive woods in Oriental or Louis XVI style, all with gilt ornamentation. Other new additions included a writing room decorated with palm trees that offered the services of a stenographer to type correspondence and, at the end of the last car, a saloon with windows overlooking a verandah with wrought nickel and brass railings. An all white-and-gilt bridal suite was the crowning extravagance.

One passenger described the saloon with admiration: "It provides a buffet and all the luxury of an elegant, up-to-date club. There are daily papers, magazines and books on the tables, and facilities are at hand for those who care to play cards, chess or other games. Stock Exchange quotations are, with other items of commercial and general news, regularly supplied to the train at its stopping places. Passengers further have the advantage of a hair-dressing salon, and there are bathrooms for ladies and gentlemen, equipped with the most approved accessories."

Trains such as the *Pennsylvania Limited* were popular only among the extremely wealthy, and in fact, most of the decoration and services were devised with influential businessmen and politicians in mind. Hard as it is to imagine, even fancier cars were custom built by the truly powerful elite (to the tune of up to a quarter million dollars each — an astonishing amount of money in the 1920s!). J. P. Morgan's private car had marble baths, Venetian mirrors, and an open, log-burning fireplace. Jay Gould traveled in a four-car entourage that included his own doctor and a cow for fresh milk (he had stomach problems). Rumor spread that one businessman's car was outfitted with solid gold plumbing fixtures — since gold doesn't tarnish, it was reported, the owner saved on the expense of having them polished.

A string of Limiteds were introduced in the years immediately following the *Pennsylvania Limited*, each with its own personality and style. By then, the country's major railway companies were competing with one another to set the standard for luxury rail service. Perhaps their competition let things get out of hand.

In 1902, the *Twentieth Century Limited*, probably the most famous passenger train in U.S. history, made its debut. It was made by the Wagner Company for the New York Central Railroad and traveled the popular run between New York and Chicago. After a few test runs, it made the 908-mile journey in an incredible twenty hours. The Penn Railroad's *Pennsylvania Limited* competed on the same route. The two trains egged each other on until the shortest time between the cities was down to eighteen hours. In the late 1920s, just before the Great Depression, business on the *Century* was so good that the New York Central made $10 million per year on that train alone.

In 1948, the New York Central unveiled the *Twentieth Century Limited,* which became one of the most elegant trains ever. It ran between New York and Chicago and offered every modern convenience to its socially proper clientele.

The Santa Fe and its Indian image

The route of the Atchison, Topeka and Santa Fe Railroad brought it into close contact with many Native American populations of the Southwest. The railroad took advantage of that fact by incorporating Indian themes into its public image. The emblem of Santa Fe passenger service was a young Navajo boy named "Chico." Chico's job in national advertising campaigns was to give the message that just as a young kid never loses his fascination with passenger trains, neither did the management of the Santa Fe Railway. Deluxe Santa Fe passenger trains were always named "Chief" — for example, the *San Francisco Chief* or the *Super Chief.* And company advertising promotions often included an invitation for passengers to tour the Native American villages of Arizona and New Mexico.

Throughout its history, the Santa Fe Railroad also had large numbers of American Indians on its payrolls, especially members of southwestern nations such as the Navajo, Apache, and Mojave. There were many, most of them working on track crews and in section gangs, and all of them paid low wages. In 1952, a total of 13,704 Indians were working for various railroads in the United States, more than half of them on the Santa Fe and most of them Navajos. By 1966, some line crews were more than 90 percent Navajo. While they were primarily employed in the Southwest, they were sometimes transferred within the system, to the Southeast and to Chicago, wherever their skills were required.

A chapter in railroad nostalgia: The bicycle railroads

In 1892, the Mount Holly & Smithville Bicycle Railroad in New Jersey was the first of its kind to be unveiled to the American public. Intended as a quiet, nonpolluting way for Mount Holly residents to commute to their jobs at the bustling H. B. Smith Manufacturing Company exactly 1.8 miles away, it was never regarded as much more than a novelty. Three thousand people rode it in the first week, but probably more for the scenery. It crossed the Rancocas Creek ten times in one mile.

The bicycles ran on a track that resembled a fence, with an inverted T-rail laid upon the top rail of the fence in which the grooved bicycle wheels fit. A major problem with the line was that it had no double tracking, so one had to dismount and remove the bike to let another rider pass. Eventually, turntables and switching spurs were included to ease the flow of traffic. Still, the Mount Holly line was never really a success, and it officially closed in 1898.

After the Mount Holly line was introduced, bicycle railroads were built along the beaches in Atlantic City and Ocean City, New Jersey, for recreational purposes. On these lines, riders were suspended on a seat eight feet off the ground with the wheels engaged on a track overhead. These lines were also short-lived, because regular bicycles were just coming into vogue and people preferred to ride wherever they wanted to go rather than on a track.

The World Wars

In 1917, just as riders were enjoying the growing pleasures of rail travel, the country became involved in World War I. In order to centrally coordinate the dramatic increase in rail traffic, especially of troops and supplies, the federal government established the Railroad Administration, a government agency, to take over running the nation's railroads. The move was a disaster, according to all involved. For just over two years, the government ran a sketchy schedule of service while losing $2 million per day.

When the war ended, the railroads went back into the hands of their former managers, who quickly sorted out the chaotic service and did a much better job of treating the passengers right. When the U.S. entered World War II in 1941, the government didn't make the same mistake again. This time, trains remained in private hands and successfully handled 90 percent of all government freight and 97 percent of all troop movements. That was no small feat considering that, compared to their prewar levels, freight traffic doubled during the war and passenger traffic quadrupled. Not only did the private companies do a better job serving the war effort, but they also contributed almost $3 million per day to the federal treasury in income taxes.

Just to give an idea of the magnitude of personnel and equipment transfer during the war, moving one infantry division of fifteen

During World War II, troops were moved entirely by train. These exhausted soldiers (below) made beds out of whatever was available as they were transported in July 1945.

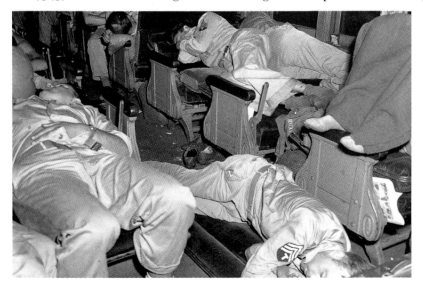

thousand men (there were eighty-nine such divisions in the U.S. Army) required forty-eight passenger trains of sixteen cars per train, with two kitchen cars each, and twenty freight trains of fifty to sixty cars each. That's why traffic was so heavy during wartime.

Another Chapter to Regulation

The Interstate Commerce Commission, the government agency established in 1887, was intended to monitor the railroads, especially their practice of giving rebates to favored shippers and of charging higher rates for non-competitive routes. While it was never given enough authority to enforce the restrictions it enacted, Congress did pass the Hepburn Act in 1906, which gave the commission more power, and also passed the Transportation Act of 1920, which empowered the commission to regulate virtually every aspect of railroading.

At the time these laws were passed, the railroad companies enjoyed a near monopoly of intercity freight transport in the U.S. But their days of such power were numbered. Trucks and airplanes would soon compete for freight trans-

Women and the Railroads

In 1874, the Santa Fe Railroad hired its first female employee, a Mrs. Caroline Prentis, as a clerk in Topeka, Kansas. By 1925, two thousand women worked for the railroad, mostly as clerical help or stenographers. Eventually they became station agents, signal tower operators, yard clerks, and even machinists. By 1942, in the middle of World War II, more than thirty-five hundred women were hired by the Santa Fe Railroad, one-third of them in jobs previously held by men. When the men returned from war, the Santa Fe asked many women to stay on, and many did. The company even created a separate women's personnel department to encourage women to consider a career in railroading. Still, women rarely rose very high in the ranks, and as late as 1972, only a few were in executive positions.

portation. In fact, by 1970, the railroads transported only 37 percent of the freight market. What followed in the 1970s was a number of railroad company bankruptcies that brought the plight of the nation's rail system to the attention of the federal government. In an effort to make the railroads more competitive — really, to keep them alive — Congress passed the Railroad Revitalization and Regulatory Reform Act of 1976 (the "4R Act"). But that wasn't enough; the companies continued to scale back service and delay repairs on track and equipment, still losing money hand over fist.

In 1980, President Carter signed the Staggers Rail Act, which undid previous regulatory laws by making rates subject to market forces once again. The effect of this law has been to give freight railroads a better chance to compete with truck and air transportation. Today, railroads transport a significant amount (37.5 percent) of the nation's freight, and service is improving all the time. In recent years, a partnership between rail and truck service was struck to bring better service to businesses at reasonable rates.

Declining Passenger Service

When most people speak of trains, they have passenger service in mind. Truth is, passenger service has always been the smaller part of railroad business. Even during World War II, when Americans turned to trains in record numbers, largely because of gas rationing, only 24 percent of rail business was in passenger service. That figure eventually fell to as low as 3 percent. Once World War II was over, passenger ridership began its steady decline. Private automobiles were the new rage. Roads and highways were built linking all major — and even not-so-major — cities. These public highways were built with government money and paid for by taxes.

As air travel developed, government subsidies funded the building of airports across the country. Railroads economized as much as they could by cutting out routes that weren't profitable and switching from steam to diesel engines, which were far more economical. But nothing seemed to keep them in the game. The railroads complained that they were being shut out by unfair government subsidies to highway and air traffic. They argued that they had never received that kind of help, at least not in the twentieth century.

The dawn of jet travel took another bite out of railroad business. Business people who had previously relied on railroad sleeping-car service to get them to their meetings could now save precious hours traveling by plane. No matter how much advertising or streamlining the trains did, they continued to lose out to planes and automobiles. In the fateful year of 1971, the federal government stepped in again, this time to salvage a basic network of passenger service before the railroad companies ended it altogether. The National Railroad Passenger Corporation, otherwise known as Amtrak, has been serving the small percentage of Americans who prefer trains ever since.

In 1944, private railroad companies together operated 20,000 daily trains. By contrast, Amtrak now runs 250 intercity trains each day. People who travel by train today know that the elaborate service and luxurious cars of the past are gone but train travel is still a safe, clean, efficient way to travel.

Railroads and Popular Culture

Railroad history — as it was being made and to this day — seeped into just about every form of American popular culture. Because of their intense romantic appeal and imagery, railroads have been and will always be an important part of the nation's history.

Heroes of Story and Song. Wallace Saunders was a Black man who never learned to read and write. He worked in the roundhouse of the Illinois Central Railroad in Canton, Mississippi, where he looked after the engines, polishing them and keeping them ready to go. While he worked, he often made up songs about working on the railroad. One of the songs he created — about the wreck that killed engineer Casey Jones — became the most popular of all railroad ballads, though Saunders never got credit for it.

> Come all you rounders if you want to hear,
> The story told about a brave engineer. . .

Because he was illiterate, he couldn't write the songs on paper, so he just kept them in his head and sang them when he and his railroading buddies got together. Another Illinois Central engineer heard Saunders sing the tale and took a liking to it. He offered Saunders a bottle of gin if he would let him write down the lyrics. Saunders accepted and sang the song over and over for him until he had both the words and the melody on paper. Three years after Casey Jones died, Saunders's ballad appeared in public, with the words and melody somewhat changed and with the names of two men Saunders didn't even know as authors of the words and music. These men made money for the song; Saunders never got a penny.

As the story goes, Casey Jones (His real name was John Luther Jones, but he was from Cayce, South Carolina, and so nicknamed Casey) was an engineer on *Cannonball No. 382*, an Illinois Central locomotive. On April 29, 1900, Casey and his African-American fireman, Sim Webb, were assigned a run from Memphis, Tennessee, to Canton, Ohio. Another engineer was supposed to do the job, but he was sick. The train was an hour and a half late. Casey tried to make up the time and was going quite fast, when up ahead he saw the rear lights of a freight train on his track. The freight hadn't pulled far enough into a sidetrack. But it was too late for Casey to stop. Casey told Webb to jump just before the crash, which he did, but Casey stayed on to try to stop his locomotive. In doing so, he saved the lives of dozens of passengers who may have died if the wreck had been worse.

> Fireman jumped but Casey stayed on;
> He was a good engineer, but he's dead and gon'.

In another famous legend, the main character, John Henry, was a newly freed slave from North Carolina who went to work for the Chesapeake & Ohio Railroad in West Virginia in 1870 or so. He was a powerful man — six feet tall, two hundred pounds — and was said to be able to drive steel on the railroad with a hammer in each hand. He died in a competition against a new steam drill, trying to prove he could do a better job. He won — but the enormous effort killed him.

> When John Henry was a little boy,
> He was sitting on his papa's knee;
> He was looking down on a piece of steel,
> Say's "A steel-drivin' man I'll be, Lord, Lord,
> A steel-drivin' man I'll be."

Then later:

> The steam drill set on the right-hand side,
> John Henry was on the left.
> He said, "I will beat that steam drill down
> Or hammer my fool self to death."

An engineer at the turn of the century, Casey Jones is remembered as a hero for sacrificing his life to save dozens of passengers and crew when his train slammed into a supposedly sidelined freight train in Mississippi in 1900. A musical comedy show entitled *Casy Jones, the Brave Engineer* appeared in 1901.

Kate Shelley's heroic act

Kate Shelley was the fifteen-year-old daughter of a Chicago & North Western Railway man. One stormy night in 1881, she was looking out her bedroom window, watching a locomotive push slowly onto a trestle bridge spanning a creek swollen from weeks of rain. Kate knew this was a pilot locomotive, sent ahead to test the bridges before the faster and heavier *Atlantic Express* came through.

As Kate watched in horror, the bridge under the test locomotive began to sag and then gave away. The engine plunged into the water, taking four crewmen with it.

Two were swept away in the raging current, but two clung to the trees for their lives. Kate's father and all the local railroad men were already out repairing track damaged by the storm. There was no one to help.

Except Kate. She knew what she had to do. She had to warn the engineer of the *Atlantic Express* or hundreds of passengers would be killed. She would have to walk to the nearest station, in Moingona, on the other side of the Des Moines River. To get there, she would have to cross a 550-foot trestle bridge, hopping from tie to tie.

She set out with a lantern. She was halfway across the bridge when the wind extinguished her light. With only lightning to help her see, she crept across the bridge, knowing that if she missed a tie or slipped, she would fall to her death. Kate reached Moingona and told the station agent about the fallen bridge. He was able to flag down the *Atlantic Express* in time. He also sent a locomotive to retrieve the men who had survived the crash of the pilot engine.

Kate Shelley received national attention for her brave deed. Railroaders everywhere sang her praises. A memorial fountain was built for her in Dubuque, Iowa. She is a lasting part of railroad history.

Legends and songs like these were created by railroad men to tell their story and make time pass. Railroading history is full of them. There are songs about building the transcontinental lines out in the parching desert or in the snow-filled mountain canyons, songs about locomotives by their engineers, songs about train wrecks and robbers and just about anything having to do with the railroads.

For us today, these recorded moments help us understand what it was like to work in a railroad-building crew or in the cab of an engine. They especially help us understand what it was like as a new immigrant come to work the roads or as an African-American — or a Chinese or other foreigner — having to accept poor treatment by their white bosses.

Hobos, Tramps, and Bums. Another well-known and colorful part of railroad culture is the hobo. From the very beginning of railroads, there were people who rode the trains without paying, usually in or on top of boxcars. They also sometimes rode on the "blind," a small platform just behind the locomotive and before the baggage car. Engineers and firemen usually had their eyes forward, so they often never noticed them. The really gutsy — and skinny — ones rode the "rods," an eighteen-inch ledge underneath the car, just one foot off the rails. If they ever fell, that was the end of them.

Hobos were very clever in their tricks to avoid being caught, but often, the engineer or crew knew they were there and just let them ride. Sometimes the crew would make them pay a small fee, what they called a tariff, that they probably put right into their pockets. But sometimes hobos stole or damaged the freight, and some got injured and then tried to sue the railroad companies.

Those types were a constant headache for railroad managers, and many tried hard to keep them off their trains.

For the most part, hobos were migrant workers moving from job to job who couldn't afford the fare. While we might use the terms "tramp" or "bum" to refer to the same people, there is a difference. According to one man who lived off and on in hobo camps, they were all migrants, but with some distinctions. A hobo, he said, works and wanders; a tramp dreams and wanders; and a bum drinks and wanders. Another saying goes like this: A hobo will work, a tramp won't, and a bum can't. The tramps and bums were the ones who caused more trouble to the railroad managers. In the 1890s, it was estimated that sixty thousand of these wanderers rode the rails in America.

While many of these people were just down on their luck or at a bad point in their lives, others actually preferred the free-ranging lifestyle of a hobo. They enjoyed seeing the country by rail, they enjoyed the companionship of the hobo "jungles," they enjoyed the lack of structure in their lives. As soon as they began to be noticed, caricatures of them appeared in magazines, newspapers, and theater productions. The cartoon hobo — a man with an unshaven, dirty face holding a stick on his shoulder from which hangs a bandana carrying all his worldly possessions — is etched in our minds, but who knows how many hobos actually looked like that.

And hobos were not all men; there were female hobos, too, though not many. Boxcar Bertha was one. She estimated that around 1930 there were one and a half million hobos, and perhaps one-half percent of them were women and girls. (If her estimate was correct, that would make seventy-five thousand female hobos.) With so many hobos, the railroad companies stepped up their efforts to rid their cars of these people, hiring special railroad police to find them and scare them enough, verbally and often physically, to keep them from coming back.

Hobos are not just a part of history; thousands of retired hobos and hundreds of modern-day hobos communicate through the National Hobo

Wearing two coats and two hats and carrying all his possessions in this 1952 photo, hobo Mike Wallace claimed to have traveled free on the railroad for thirty-nine years.

Railroad language we use today

All sorts of terms and phrases we commonly use today have their origin in railroading. Have you ever been "sidetracked" or "derailed" from something you were doing, or did you ever stop in midsentence because you lost your "train" of thought? Has anyone ever accused you of being "asleep at the switch"? Were you disappointed when you didn't "make the grade"?

People use these terms freely without realizing their true meanings. To live life on the "fast track" is an expression we understand, but do we stop to think that it was originally used to refer to the tracks used only for express trains?

Association and through the *Hobo Times,* a bimonthly newsletter that is published in Los Angeles. Some even get out there and ride today's freight trains.

The Future of Railroads

In some densely populated areas of the country, especially New England and Chicago, commuter trains run by private companies have been able to stay

alive and even prosper. They cater to business people traveling from outlying areas into the downtown districts of cities such as New York, Boston, and Philadelphia. These trains succeed partly because traffic in these cities is so heavy, and parking so expensive, that people prefer not to drive.

While most short-line commuter trains will probably continue to survive, many Americans have questioned why the federal government continues to subsidize Amtrak's passenger trains when they lose millions of dollars each year. Though ridership has risen significantly in the past decade, the numbers aren't big enough to justify such financial losses, they say. Those who do take trains believe they should never disappear. Many people are afraid of flying and need the train. Other train advocates believe that with the new high-speed, fuel-efficient trains that are being designed, railroads may be the key to future transportation. They are cleaner and can ease traffic congestion in major cities. In France and Japan, increasing numbers of people ride very modern trains that can go as fast as three hundred miles per hour.

In fact, in 1993, Amtrak experimented with a Swedish train on its Boston-New York-Washington, D.C., route. The German- designed InterCity Express (ICE) trains have also been test-run in the United States. But the problem is with an aging track system that can't accommodate the high speeds these ultramodern trains are capable of. Federal and state governments would have to commit enormous sums of money to upgrade and reroute tracks before these trains could work in the U.S. Because the federal government hasn't taken the

initiative to consider a new nationwide system, many states (such as Texas and Ohio) and cities (such as Los Angeles and Pittsburgh) have been considering their own proposals for years; some are getting close to implementing plans that involve trains going speeds of up to 250 miles per hour.

It remains to be seen how pervasive a role trains will play in the nation's future. But their role in its past is indisputable. What would the United States look like today if trains hadn't come along when they did? Not only did the railroads extend the United States from coast to coast and build a truly national economy, but they also brought hundreds of thousands of immigrants to our shores — either to do the grueling work of building the railroad lines or in search of a new life farming the open prairie. The railroads were tough on many groups of people: the low-paid, poorly treated ethnic laborers, the farmers paying freight charges that kept them tied by poverty to the land, the African-American train porters kept in a state of servitude. Perhaps the most shameful legacy of the railroads is how they displaced and destroyed the hundreds of Native American cultures living here before the coming of the white man. It is an understatement to say that the railroads changed the face of America — permanently, for better or for worse.

Above: This railroad yard routes freight traffic with the help of elevated track.

Opposite page, top to bottom: Commuter trains can ease urban auto congestion; a Union Pacific Dispatch Center in Omaha keeps track of trains with high-tech computers; German Inter-City Express (ICE) trains are being considered for use in the U.S. but would require significant track upgrading.

Left: Many Americans still love to ride — or even watch — trains as they roll through the countryside. Can passenger trains survive in today's world of autos and airplanes? Time will tell.

1814   Englishman George Stephenson develops the first steam locomotive

1825   In the U.S., Colonel John Stevens presents his twelve-foot "steam waggon" on a circular track on New Jersey estate; it was America's first locomotive and ran at twelve miles per hour; on September 17, Stephenson's steam engine powers the world's first freight train on the twenty-five-mile Stockton & Darlington Railroad in Britain; *Locomotion No. 1* pulls thirty-five cars at twelve miles per hour; in October, the Erie Canal is completed, revolutionizing freight transport, until railroads prove even better and cheaper

1827   The first U.S. railroad charter is granted to the Baltimore & Ohio Railroad

1829   Horatio Allen brings four British locomotives to the United States; the *Stourbridge Lion* makes its first — and only — run

1830   T-shaped rail is designed by Camden & Amboy President Robert L. Stevens; in August, the *Tom Thumb* races against horse-drawn rail car to prove the power of steam locomotives; on Christmas Day, the *Best Friend of Charleston* makes its debut

1831   U.S. mail transported for first time by rail, in South Carolina; in June, six months after its debut, the *Best Friend of Charleston* explodes, killing its fireman; first railroad tragedy, creating a public relations and image problem for railroads

1850   Asa Whitney receives support from eighteen state legislatures for his transcontinental plan

1861   Civil War breaks out; South is at a disadvantage because two-thirds of America's tracks are in the North, enabling faster troop and ammunitions movement

1862   Pacific Railroad Act signed into law by President Abraham Lincoln; the law authorizes two railroads — the Central Pacific (CP) and the Union Pacific (UP) — to build the nation's first transcontinental line

1867   American Indians resist European-American encroachment on native lands in year of worst wars between Native Americans and whites

1868   First automatic coupler invented by Major Eli Janney, a former Confederate officer

1869   George Westinghouse invents the first air brakes, required on all trains by 1893; on April 28, Chinese CP crews break track-laying record by setting more than ten miles in one day; on May 10, Central Pacific and Union Pacific lines meet at Promontory, Utah

1881   Second transcontinental line completed along the southern route

1887   Interstate Commerce Act signed into law; freight rates become regulated

1893   Safety Appliance Act requires all trains to be equipped with automatic couplers and air brakes

1902   *Twentieth Century Limited*, the most lavish Pullman train in history, hits the New York Central's tracks for runs between New York and Chicago

1906   The Hepburn Act gives the ICC more regulatory power, including setting maximum freight rates

1916   Peak of railroad use in U.S. with a total of 254,000 miles of track

1917   President Woodrow Wilson places the railroads under government control to help with increased wartime traffic; this lasts twenty-six months, during which the government loses $2 million per day

1918   Standard Time Act is approved by Congress, greatly improving scheduled rail service

1920   Transportation Act gives the ICC power to regulate all aspects of railroading

1925	The Brotherhood of Sleeping Car Porters, the nation's first African-American union, is established
1933	The Delaware & Hudson lays the first continuous welded rail, ending the clickety-clack sound
1934	The Chicago, Burlington & Quincy is the first railroad to use diesel engines for passenger service
1971	The National Railroad Passenger Corporation, otherwise known as Amtrak, steps in with government subsidies to keep money-losing private companies from ending passenger service altogether
1976	The Railroad Revitalization and Regulatory Reform Act (the "4R Act") becomes law, undoing much of earlier rate regulation so that market forces take over
1980	President Carter signs the Staggers Rail Act, making railroad rates determined more by market forces than by regulation

GLOSSARY

advocate	somebody who believes strongly in — and works on behalf of — a cause
Amtrak	the nickname for the National Railroad Passenger Corporation, created in 1971 by the federal government to operate passenger trains in the U.S. when private companies could no longer afford to do so
brakeman	a railroad employee who helps the conductor and checks, operates, and repairs the train's brakes
Brotherhood of Sleeping Car Porters	the nation's first all-African-American union, formed in 1925 by Pullman sleeping-car porters; this group of porters, all of them African-American, had been excluded from the American Railway Union, which was organized by Eugene V. Debs in the nineteenth century to represent white Pullman workers
Celestial	a term applied to the Chinese immigrants because they called their homeland the Celestial Kingdom
couple	to connect two rail cars together
Credit Mobilier	the name of a "dummy" company set up by Union Pacific boss Thomas Durant during the Great Race; by depositing government money intended for the railroad into the Credit Mobilier, he was able to amass a personal fortune while the Union Pacific went deeper and deeper into debt
Debs, Eugene V.	one of America's first labor organizers; he instigated railroad workers to strike in 1894
fireman	the second man (besides the engineer) in the steam engine's cab; he feeds coal into the fire to make steam
gauge	the distance between the rails of a train track
grade	the uphill slope of railroad tracks
Granger	the nickname for a member of the National Patrons of Husbandry, the farmers' group that protested unfair railroad rates in the 1870s
the Great Race	the nickname for the building of the nation's first transcontinental railroad; the Great Race pitted the Central Pacific (primarily Chinese crews building eastward from Sacramento) and the Union Pacific (primarily Irish crews building westward from Omaha) in a race to see which company could lay the most track, and make the most money, before eventually hooking up in Promontory Summit, Utah

Interstate Commerce Act	(Interstate Commerce Commission) the law that created a government committee to set rules for trading merchandise over state borders
Iron Horse	a nickname for a railroad locomotive; used frequently to describe the early engines that pulled cars, men, and equipment over the Great Plains and through Indian country during the building of the transcontinental railroads
Johnson bar or lever	the reverse handle used by the engineer on a locomotive
Mennonite	a member of a sect of Anabaptist Christians begun in the sixteenth century; characterized by the simplicity of their way of life and belief in nonviolence as a way of resolving disputes
migrant	a person who moves from place to place, calling no place "home"
Pacific Railroad Act (1862)	the federal law that settled the ongoing debate in Congress over which companies would complete the country's first railroad from Omaha, Nebraska, to the Pacific Ocean, as well as the route
Pullman porters	Employees of the Pullman Palace Car Company, by 1927 the nation's largest manufacturer of elegant railroad sleeping cars; the first of what would become an all-Black legion of Pullman porters were hired in the 1850s, and by the 1890s, nearly twenty thousand Black porters were on the company's payroll, making it the nation's largest — although not always the most fair — employer of African-Americans
roundhouse	the building in a railroad yard where locomotives are repaired and housed; each locomotive is on a track that leads to the turntable
switch	a device with a movable piece of rail that moves a train from one track to another
Trail of Tears	the forced march of between thirteen thousand and sixteen thousand Cherokee from their homes in Florida to Indian Territory (present-day Oklahoma) in 1838; at least four thousand perished during this march, one of many suffered by American Indians as the U.S. government pursued its policy of removing Indians west
transcontinental	a train line that crossed the entire span of the continent
turntable	a revolving piece of track that is used to turn engines around
union	a group of laborers who join together to negotiate work terms with their bosses

FURTHER READING

Armstrong, Virginia Irving, compiler. *I Have Spoken: American History Through the Voices of the Indians*. Athens: Swallow Press/Ohio University Press, 1971, 1991.

Brown, Dee. *Hear That Lonesome Whistle Blow: Railroads in the West*. New York: Holt, Rhinehart & Winston, 1977.

Brown, Dee. *Wondrous Times on the Frontier*. New York: Harper Collins, 1992.

Fisher, Leonard Everett. *Tracks Across America: The Story of the American Railroad, 1825-1900*. New York: Holiday House, 1992.

McKissack, Patricia and Frederick. *A Long Hard Journey: The Story of the Pullman Porter*. New York: Walker & Co., 1989.

Nabokov, Peter. *Native American Testimony (A Chronicle of Indian-White Relations from Prophecy to the Present, 1492-1992)*. New York: Viking Penguin, 1991.

Press, Petra. *A Multicultural Portrait of the Move West*. New York: Marshall Cavendish Corporation, 1994.

White, Richard. *It's Your Misfortune and None of My Own: A New History of the American West*. Norman: University of Oklahoma Press, 1991.

Zinn, Howard. *A People's History of the United States*. New York: Harper & Row, 1980.